WALKING

ISTANBUL

THE BEST OF THE CITY

Tristan Rutherford &
Kathryn Tomasetti

NATIONAL GEOGRAPHIC

Washington, D.C.

WALKING ISTANBUL

CONTENTS

PART
1

PAGE 12
WHIRLWIND TOURS

Previous pages: Eminönü shoreline; left: street life around the Galata Tower; right: Obelisk of Theodosius; above right: Turkish ceramic; bottom right: backstreet in Çukurcuma.

PART
2

PAGE 46
ISTANBUL'S NEIGHBORHOODS

PART
3

PAGE 174
TRAVEL ESSENTIALS

Introduction

As a lifelong resident of Istanbul, I've never considered living anywhere else. Just as love is an addiction so, too, is life in Istanbul. All worries are washed away with one passionate kiss—a quiet walk on the Galata Bridge over the Golden Horn; a stroll in front of the Historic Peninsula, the epicenter of four major empires; or a saunter through the pine-shaded roads of the Princes Islands overlooking the Sea of Marmara.

Indeed, the best way to enjoy this vibrant city is on foot, and you can expect plenty of surprises, such as an Ottoman-era monument integrated into the modern cityscape or the tulips carved into the facade of Topkapı Palace's Sultanahmet Fountain. Then there are the flamboyant shades of color punctuating the scenes around you: the incredible motley mix of flowers sold on street corners, the changing blues of the two seas that surround the city, the golden glimmer of candlelight at cafés on the Bosporus. As you explore, you'll be tempted by such gastronomic pleasures as *simit*—the traditional bagel-like pastry with sesame seeds—or a glass of wine produced by a still unknown but expert Turkish winemaker. Is it any wonder that this city has inspired notions of love through the ages?

The dome of the Süleymaniye Mosque rises above the narrow streets of the bazaar neighborhood.

Dr. Gül İrepoğlu
Art historian, architect, author

Visiting Istanbul

With buildings representing 1,500 years of history and a series of neighborhoods that each has its own unique charm, Istanbul brims with fascinating sights. Ancient trades and traditions live on in the city's intimate courtyards (hans), while a thriving arts scene guarantees a host of hip galleries, museums, and cafés.

Istanbul in a Nutshell

Istanbul straddles the Bosporus waterway that separates Europe from Asia. Founded as Byzantium in the seventh century B.C., the city later became the center of, first, the Byzantine, and then, the Ottoman Empire. Under the Byzantines, the city was named Constantinople. Although the Ottomans preferred Istanbul, the name was not adopted in the West until the 20th century. Both empires have left their mark. Numerous ancient sites cluster in the Old City, two striking palaces grace the shores of the Bosporus—one on each side—and the hilly skyline is dotted with numerous mosques and towers. Mercantile roots established under Sultan Mehmet II in the mid-15th century live on in the many markets that thrive here, notably the Grand Bazaar and Spice Market.

Istanbul Day-by-Day

The following list shows when sights are closed: Some close for half or full days during religious festivals (see p. 176). These are moveable feasts, so check websites for details.

Monday Beylerbeyi Palace; Dolmabahçe Palace; Great Palace Mosaic Museum; Hagia Sophia; Istanbul Archaeology Museums; Istanbul Modern; Maritime Museum; Museum of Innocence; Museum of Turkish & Islamic Art; Panorama 1453; Pera Museum; SALT Galata; Vakıflar Carpet Museum; Whirling Dervish Hall.

Tuesday Hagia Eirene; Museum of the History of Science & Technology in Islam; Topkapı Palace; Yıldız Palace.

Wednesday Chora Church; Rumeli Fortress.

Thursday Beylerbeyi Palace; Dolmabahçe Palace.

Friday Blue Mosque; Süleymaniye Mosque; Yeraltı Mosque; Mihrimah Sultan Mosque; Şakirin Mosque; Atik Valide Mosque.

Saturday and Sunday All sights are open.

Passing the neoclassical Büyük Mecidiye Mosque, in Ortaköy, on a Bosporus ferry tour

Navigating Istanbul

Within each neighborhood, with very few exceptions, all key sights are easily reached on foot. This is particularly true of the Old City, Galata, Karaköy, and Beyoğlu, where sights are found in close proximity. That said, Istanbul has a very efficient public transportation network (see p. 177) that allows you to travel easily between neighborhoods, particularly if you buy an **İstanbulkart** (see p. 177), which includes a discount on the already cheap fares and can be used on all transporation—trams (including the historic trams), buses, ferries, and the Metro.

Istanbul's Religion

Turkey is a predominantly Sunni Muslim country. Its mosques are working mosques and, five times a day, you'll hear the mesmerizing call to prayer echo throughout the city. The country is also a secular republic, however, which means that religious practices are moderate. Non-Muslims are welcome everywhere in Istanbul, including its many mosques. Bear in mind that when you visit a mosque, you must remove your shoes and leave them outside. Women are asked to cover their heads—for which scarves are provided—shoulders, and knees.

Using This Guide

Each tour—which might be only a walk, or might take advantage of the city's public transportation as well—is plotted on a map and has been planned to take into account opening hours and the times of day when sites are less crowded. Many end near restaurants or lively nightspots for evening activities.

Whirlwind Tours

Whirlwind Tours are for people who have only a day or weekend and want to be sure that they see the best. Choose a tour based on your time and interests: A Day; A Weekend (Day 1 & Day 2); For Fun; For History Lovers; For Foodies; and With Kids (Day 1 & Day 2).

Tips For the Day and Weekend Tours, a "tips" spread following the itinerary map provides insider information on detours from the key sites, extra places to see, nearby cafés and restaurants, and ideas for adapting the tours to suit your interests.

Site Descriptions
For each of the Whirlwind Tours, a key sites spread follows the map spread, providing descriptions of all the sites and practical information for visitors.

Neighborhood Tours

The seven neighborhood tours each begin with an introduction, followed by an itinerary map highlighting the key sites that make up the tour and detailed key sites descriptions. Each tour is followed by an "in-depth" spread showcasing one major site along the route, a "distinctly" Istanbul spread providing background information on a quintessential element of that neighborhood, and a "best of" spread that groups sites thematically.

Itinerary Map A map of the neighborhood shows the locations of the key sites, Metro stations, and main streets.

Captions These blurbs briefly describe the key sites and give instructions on finding the next site on the tour. Page references direct you to full descriptions of the sites on the following pages.

Route

Price Ranges for Key Sites

$	TL10 and less
$$	TL11–20
$$$	TL21–40
$$$$	TL41 and above

Price Ranges for Good Eats (for one person, excluding drinks)

$	Less than TL25
$$	TL25 to 50
$$$	TL50 to 100
$$$$	TL100 to 200
$$$$$	over TL200

Key Sites Descriptions These spreads provide a detailed description and highlights for each site, following the order on the map, plus its address, phone number, days closed, entrance fee, nearest Metro and tram stops, and website.

Good Eats Refer to these lists for a selection of cafés and restaurants along the tour.

USING THIS GUIDE

PART 1

Whirlwind Tours

Istanbul in a Day

*This compact tour of the Old City's major sights ends
with stunning views across the Golden Horn.*

5 Grand Bazaar (see pp. 80–83)
Have fun scouring the avenues for
bargains in this atmospheric covered
market. Exit the marketplace
through Mahmutpaşa Kapısı, and
walk downhill toward the waterfront.

4 Blue Mosque (see pp. 54–55) As
you tour the mosque grounds,
take a peek inside the
Sultan's Pavilion and visit
Sultan Ahmed I's tomb.
Exit to the north and
follow Divan Yolu
Caddesi west.

6 Galata Bridge (see pp. 113–114) Order a refreshing
aperitif, sit back, and watch the ferries chug across
the Golden Horn as you wait for the sun to set.

Haliç

6 Galata Bridge
(Galata Köprüsü)

Eminönü

EMİNÖNÜ

0   400 meters

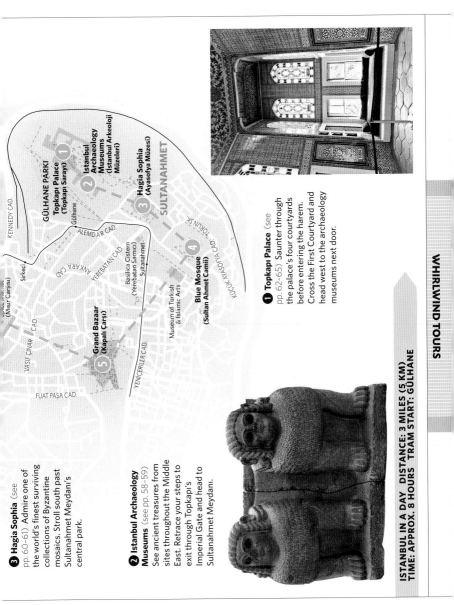

3 Hagia Sophia (see pp. 60–61) Admire one of the world's finest surviving collections of Byzantine mosaics. Stroll south past Sultanahmet Meydanı's central park.

2 Istanbul Archaeology Museums (see pp. 58–59) See ancient treasures from sites throughout the Middle East. Retrace your steps to exit through Topkapı's Imperial Gate and head to Sultanahmet Meydanı.

1 Topkapı Palace (see pp. 62–65) Saunter through the palace's four courtyards before entering the harem. Cross the First Courtyard and head west to the archaeology museums next door.

GÜLHANE PARKI

Topkapı Palace (Topkapı Sarayı) ①

Istanbul Archaeology Museums (İstanbul Arkeoloji Müzeleri) ②

Hagia Sophia (Ayasofya Müzesi) ③

SULTANAHMET

Blue Mosque (Sultan Ahmet Camii) ④

Museum of Turkish & Islamic Arts

Basilica Cistern (Yerebatan Sarnıcı)

Grand Bazaar (Kapalı Çarşı) ⑤

KENNEDY CAD.

Sirkeci

ALEMDAR CAD.

Gülhane

ANKARA CAD.

YEREBATAN CAD.

Sultanahmet

KÜÇÜK AYASOFYA CAD. TORUN SK.

YENİÇERİLER CAD.

FUAT PAŞA CAD.

VASIF ÇINAR CAD.

(Mısır Çarşısı)

ISTANBUL IN A DAY DISTANCE: 3 MILES (5 KM)
TIME: APPROX. 8 HOURS TRAM START: GÜLHANE

Tips

This tour offers the best of Istanbul's Old City sights. Each is described elsewhere in the book—just follow the cross-references for more detailed information. The following tips provide advice on visiting these major locations when you have limited time and suggest alternative sights and places to eat nearby.

❶ Topkapı Palace (see pp. 62–65) The best time to visit Topkapı Palace (Topkapı Sarayı) is at the beginning of the day or at the end, since these times tend to be less popular with bus tours. On arrival, take the opportunity to get your bearings for the rest of the day from any one of the viewpoints over Istanbul's Old City neighborhood.

Gülhane Park café, overlooking the Golden Horn and the Bosporus

Note that the number of people admitted to the ■ HAREM at any one time is limited, so hit this sight early on in your visit if you can (see box p. 63).

❷ Istanbul Archaeology Museums (see pp. 58–59) Visit just the ■ MUSEUM OF ARCHAEOLOGY (Arkeoloji Müzesi) and seek out the discoveries that were made during the construction of the new sub-Bosporus Marmaray Metro line. The excavations uncovered the ancient harbor of Theodosius, complete with a wealth of shipwreck treasures—amphorae, oil lamps, and ivory. Seeking refreshment? You'll find a café in a small leafy garden beside the ■ TILE PAVILION (Çinili Köşk Müzesi), overlooking ■ GÜLHANE PARK (Gülhane Parkı; see pp. 57–58). With ancient statues poking out from amid the greenery, this makes for a pleasant place to stop for a cool drink.

❸ Hagia Sophia (see pp. 60–61)
If you're feeling hungry, there's no shortage of street-food vendors on ■ **Ayasofya Meydanı,** just outside the entrance to the Hagia Sophia (Ayasofya Müzesi)—take your pick from grilled corn on the cob, roasted chestnuts, and fresh-baked *simit* rolls (see p. 87). If the crowds are too oppressive inside the museum, take a break on the grounds outside. Here, you'll find the exquisitely tiled, 16th-century ■ **Mausoleum of Sultan Selim II,** among others. Entry is free. Walk around the corner to Bab-ı Hümayun Caddesi to find the separate entrance to the tomb area.

❹ Blue Mosque (see pp. 54–55)
En route to the Blue Mosque (Sultan Ahmet Camii), don't miss the ■ **Million Stone** (Milion Taşı; *Divan Yolu Caddesi),* a remnant from the days when Istanbul was Constantinople, the center of the Byzantine Empire. This small monument marks the point from which distances to all other major cities in the empire were measured.

❺ Grand Bazaar (see pp. 80–83)
While in the area, seek out some of the atmospheric ■ **hans** around the perimeter of the Grand Bazaar (Kapalı Çarşı). Many of these ancient trading inns are still in use by resident artisans. Stop to watch some of them as they

CUSTOMIZING **YOUR DAY**

Instead of watching the sun set from Galata Bridge, book yourself on a memorable evening cruise of the Bosporus. **Bosphorus Tours** (*tel 0554 797 2646, $$$$, bosphorustour.com*) offers a daily cruise complete with an evening meal and classic Turkish entertainments, such as traditional Turkish *katibim* music, a henna ceremony, and belly dancing. Prices include transfers to and from your hotel.

work. Favorites include the sleepy ■ **Iç Cebeci Han** in the northwest of the bazaar, in which carpets are repaired.

❻ Galata Bridge (see pp. 113–114)
Arrive at the Galata Bridge (Galata Köprüsü) in time to enjoy the city's sublime sunset. To finish your day with a fish dinner, walk to the other side of the bridge and head through ■ **Karaköy Fish Market** (Karaköy Balık Pazarı; see p. 37) to a row of alfresco fish restaurants. Try ■ **Grifin** (*Kardeşim Sokak 45, tel 0212 243 4080, $$$)* for a splashout meal with stunning views. Just south of Galata Bridge, you'll find the more traditional ■ **Liman** (*Rıhtım Caddesi 52–53, tel 0212 292 3992, $$)* on the top floor of the Yolcu Salonu just facing the Karaköy port. As well as awe-inspiring views, this restaurant has a good wine list.

DAY 1

Istanbul in a Weekend

From Byzantine art to Ottoman luxury, Istanbul's must-see sights reveal a diverse cultural history.

1 Topkapı Palace
(see pp. 62–65) Visit the Imperial Treasury to see the world-famous, jewel-encrusted dagger. Walk westward across the grassy quad to the Istanbul Archaeology Museums next door.

5 Basilica Cistern
(see pp. 56–57) Keep an eye out for the schools of carp that swim in the waters of this eerie subterranean cistern.

SİRKECİ

GÜLHANE PARKI

Sirkeci Train Station
(Sirkeci Tren Garı)

HÜDAVENDİGÂR CAD.

EBÜSSUUD CAD.

Gülhane

1 Topkapı Palace
(Topkapı Sarayı)

2 Istanbul Archaeology Museums
(İstanbul Arkeoloji Müzeleri)

④ Blue Mosque (see pp. 54–55) Spot the different colors and designs used in the many thousands of Iznik tiles. Loop northward across Sultanahmet Meydanı and on to Yerebatan Caddesi.

② Istanbul Archaeology Museums (see pp. 58–59) Admire scenes that were once part of Ishtar Gate of Babylon. Stroll back through Topkapı Palace's First Courtyard, then south to Ayasofya Meydanı.

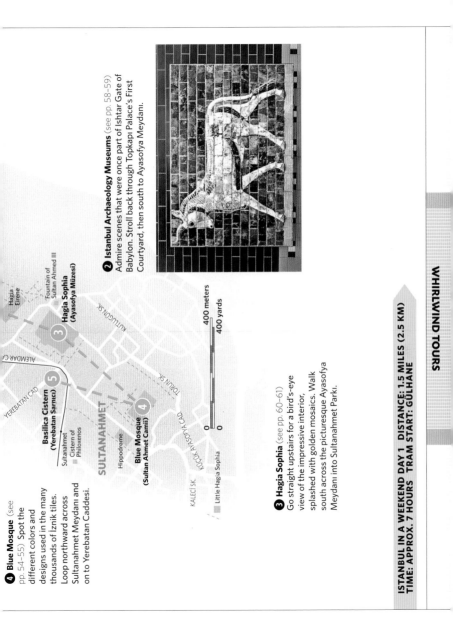

SULTANAHMET

Hagia Eirene

Fountain of Sultan Ahmed III

Hagia Sophia (Ayasofya Müzesi)

ALEMDAR C.

YEREBATAN CAD.

Basilica Cistern (Yerebatan Sarnıcı) ⑤

Sultanahmet
Cistern of Philoxenos

KUTLUGÜN SK.

Hippodrome

TORUN SK.

Blue Mosque (Sultan Ahmet Camii) ④

KÜÇÜK AYASOFYA CAD.

KALECİ SK.

Little Hagia Sophia

0 — 400 meters
0 — 400 yards

③ Hagia Sophia (see pp. 60–61) Go straight upstairs for a bird's-eye view of the impressive interior, splashed with golden mosaics. Walk south across the picturesque Ayasofya Meydanı into Sultanahmet Parkı.

WHIRLWIND TOURS

ISTANBUL IN A WEEKEND DAY 1   DISTANCE: 1.5 MILES (2.5 KM)
TIME: APPROX. 7 HOURS   TRAM START: GÜLHANE

Tips

Two days affords enough time to immerse yourself in Istanbul's diverse cultural history. Day One covers the Old City's major sights, but there is plenty of scope for improvisation. Read about the main attractions later in the book and consider the following tips for interesting alternatives and detours on the way.

WHIRLWIND TOURS

❶ Topkapı Palace (see pp. 62–65) With time being short, limit your visit to Topkapı Palace (Topkapı Sarayı) to its incredible ■ **HAREM.** If you don't have a ■ **MUSEUM PASS İSTANBUL** (see pp. 177–178), buy your ticket as soon as you arrive and tour one or two of the four courtyards until your allocated time slot. Few visitors make it to the

Hellenistic stone sculptures at the Istanbul Archaeological Museums

■ **FOURTH COURTYARD,** so this may well be the quietest. There are a number of summer pavilions in this courtyard and, in the northeast corner, a ■ **PANORAMIC TERRACE** with views across the Bosporus and the Golden Horn.

❷ Istanbul Archaeology Museums (see pp. 58–59) Focus your visit on just one of the three museums here. The ■ **TILE PAVILION** (Çinili Köşk Müzesi; see p. 105) is a manageable size. Alternatively, skip this sight altogether and step outside to ■ **GÜLHANE PARK** (Gülhane Parkı; see pp. 57–58). Picturesque year-round, the park offers a welcome break and a relaxing stroll in the open air.

❸ Hagia Sophia (see pp. 60–61) If you see just one thing at the Hagia Sophia (Ayasofya Müzesi), make sure it's the ■ **SOUTH GALLERY** (upstairs), with its stunning Byzantine mosaics. En route to the museum, just after passing through Topkapı Palace's ■ **IMPERIAL GATE,** look left and you'll see the wonderfully ornate ■ **FOUNTAIN OF SULTAN AHMED III,** a fine example of Ottoman architecture from the Tulip Period. If you're looking for lunch, try ■ **MOZAIK** (*İncili Çavuş Sokak 1, tel 0212 512 4177, $–$$*), just off Divan Yolu Caddesi, with its relaxed atmosphere, outdoor seating, and international menu. A five-minute walk west of Hagia Sophia will take you to the more traditional ■ **RUMELI CAFE** (*Ticarethane Sokak 8, tel 0212 512 0008, $$*), where Turkish ravioli (*mantı*) is a specialty.

❹ **Blue Mosque** (see pp. 54–55) Between the Hagia Sophia (Ayasofya Müzesi) and the Blue Mosque (Sultan Ahmet Camii), make time for a quick tour of ■ **THE HIPPODROME** (see p. 70), the ancient Roman racetrack around which citizens once gathered to watch charioteers compete. Not all of the sights here date from ancient times. Monuments to seek out include, at the northern end, the ■ **GERMAN FOUNTAIN,** which commemorates a visit to Istanbul made by Kaiser Wilhelm II in 1898. Look up inside the dome to see beautiful gold mosaic work. Progressing southward you'll see—

CUSTOMIZING **YOUR DAY**

If, on reaching the Basilica Cistern, you feel that you've seen enough for the day, skip this sight and treat yourself to a Turkish bath instead. At the **Cağaloğlu Hamam** (Cağaloğlu Hamamı; *Prof. Kazım İsmail Gürkan Cadessi 24, tel 0212 522 2423, $$$–$$$$*), northeast of the cistern, you can choose from a range of services that include an exfoliation treatment, a dry massage, and a foam massage. You can also opt for a combination of all three.

in the following order—the ■ **OBELISK OF THEODOSIUS** (see p. 32) and the ■ **SERPENTINE COLUMN** (Burma Sütun), both ancient spoils of war, and the ■ **CONSTANTINE COLUMN** (Örme Sütun), a fifth-century column made of stone, whose origins remain a mystery to this day.

❺ **Basilica Cistern** (see pp. 56–57) If there are long lines at the Basilica Cistern (Yerebatan Sarnıcı), walk a little farther west (no more than five minutes) on Divan Yolu Caddesi until you reach İmran Öktem Caddesi 4, home to the ■ **CISTERN OF PHILOXENOS** (Binbirdirek Sarnıcı; see p. 33). This undergeround reservoir may have fewer columns—94 fewer, to be precise—but it is no less impressive and attracts far fewer tourists.

Istanbul in a Weekend

This fun-packed day begins and ends with visits to the city's vibrant covered markets.

❶ Süleymaniye Mosque (see p. 76)
Admire the workmanship at the city's second largest mosque. Exit south of the mosque, following Fuat Paşa Caddesi and Çadırcılar Caddesi.

❷ Grand Bazaar
(see pp. 80–83)
Make your way to the market's original Byzantine trading hall. Leaving the bazaar through Mahmutpaşa Kapısı, zigzag your way downhill on Mahmutpaşa Yokuşu.

❸ Eminönü Fish Sandwich (see p. 86)
Fortify yourself with a hot fish sandwich as you perch alongside locals at one of the low stools and tables nearby. Bosporus boat tours depart from the adjacent Eminönü ferry terminal.

WHIRLWIND TOURS

ISTANBUL IN A WEEKEND DAY 2   DISTANCE: 3 MILES (5 KM)
TIME: APPROX. 9 HOURS   METRO START: VEZNECILER

7 Karaköy Dinner (see p. 25) Cap off your weekend with a contemporary Ottoman meal at upscale Turkish eatery, Lokanta Maya.

6 Galata Bridge (see pp. 113–114) Slowly stroll the western side of the bridge to take in one of the Golden Horn's famous fiery sunsets. Continue north into Karaköy, then east on Kemankeş Caddesi.

7 Karaköy Dinner

5 Spice Market (see p. 78) Immerse yourself in the sights, sounds, and smells of this ancient covered market. Retrace your steps across Ragıp Gümüşpala Caddesi.

4 Bosporus Boat Tour (see p. 25) Sit back and relax as you sail up and down the Bosporus. On returning to Eminönü, cross Ragıp Gümüşpala Caddesi heading south.

WHIRLWIND TOURS

Tips

For the second day of your weekend, consider the following tips for visiting the sights on limited time and with suggestions for detours on the way. The tour centers on a ferry-boat ride up the Bosporus and back. Use the page references provided to read about the attractions you'll pass on the way.

❶ **Süleymaniye Mosque** (see p. 76) With little time to explore the extensive grounds, dive inside the mosque to observe the fine ■ **CALLIGRAPHY** by leading artists of the day.

❷ **Grand Bazaar** (see pp. 80–83) Arrive at the Grand Bazaar (Kapalı Çarşı) knowing what you want to buy and where—■ **YAĞLIKÇILAR CADDESI** for textiles, for example—and head straight there. More interested in the

The inner courtyard at Süleymaniye Mosque

architecture? Make a beeline for ■ **İÇ BEDESTEN,** the market's elegant and original, vaulted trading hall. Outside the bazaar, flanking its eastern perimeter, is ■ **Ç. NURUOSMANIYE CADDESI,** on which you'll find a more upmarket shopping experience. Here, ■ **ARMAGGAN** (*No. 65*) is one of the city's best stores for design and jewelry.

❸ **Eminönü Fish Sandwich** (see p. 86) If a fish sandwich lacks appeal, dip into ■ **TAHTAKALE** (see p. 79), the network of streets south of Ragıp Gümüşpala Caddesi. Follow your nose—and the locals—to find a tasty döner kebab. You'll see spits rotating in many of the windows here. While in this area, don't miss Istanbul's ■ **GRAND POST OFFICE** (Büyük Postane; *Büyük Postane Caddesi 25*). Duck through the marble facade to admire the building's stained-glass and wooden interior.

④ Bosporus Boat Tour Several different ferry companies offer short tours on the Bosporus (lasting around 90 minutes), but ■ **TURYOL** (*Istanbul Eski Ticaret Odası Yanı, Park İçi, tel 0212 512 1287, $$, turyol.com*) is the only one to do so year-round. Tours leave on the hour, normally from 10 a.m. until 6 p.m., although this varies according to season and weather. Check the company website for details. You can hop on board at the Eminönü ferry terminal, just west of the ■ **GALATA BRIDGE** (Galata Köprüsü; see pp. 113–114). As the boat heads out of the Golden Horn and northward onto the Bosporus, you'll see the ■ **GALATA TOWER** (Galata Kulesi; see pp. 110–111) on your left, then the ■ **DOLMABAHÇE PALACE** (Dolmabahçe Sarayı; see pp. 152–153). The boat sails beneath the Bosporus Bridge (Boğaziçi Köprüsü) and continues north, passing the pretty waterside villages of Bebek and Arnavutköy on the left, as well as the 15th-century ■ **RUMELI FORTRESS** (Rumelihisarı; see p. 156). The boat turns around at the ■ **FATIH SULTAN MEHMET BRIDGE** (Fatih Sultan Mehmet Köprüsü, also known as the second Bosporus Bridge), and will pass the ■ **BEYLERBEYI PALACE** (Beylerbeyi Sarayı; see p. 162) on your left as you return to Eminönü.

CUSTOMIZING **YOUR DAY**

Want to finish your weekend having spent time in both European and Asian Istanbul? Skip the fish sandwich and swap the Bosporus Boat Tour for a ferry to Kadıköy *(about 20 minutes, $)*. After seeing the sights of the vibrant **Kadıköy Fish Market** (Kadıköy Balık Pazarı; see p. 166) head to **Çiya Sofrası** *(Güneşlibahçe Sokak 43, tel 0216 330 3190, $-$$)* for lunch (see pp. 166–167). You'll return to Eminönü in time to see the Spice Market and Galata sunset—even in winter.

⑤ Spice Market (see p. 78) Head to ■ **TAHMIS SOKAK** on the market's western perimeter to get in line at ■ **KURUKAHVECI MEHMET EFENDI** (*No. 66*), purveyors of Turkey's most popular coffee brand, to buy your own package—still warm from roasting. You can buy a coffee pot from a store nearby.

⑥ Galata Bridge (see pp. 113–114) The sunset from here—shimmering across the waves from crimson to ruby red—is unrivaled in all of Istanbul.

⑦ Karaköy Dinner Reserve a table at ■ **LOKANTA MAYA** (see p. 113) for outstanding modern Turkish cuisine. Instead of having dessert here, walk back on Mumhane Caddesi toward Galata Bridge and drop in at ■ **KARAKÖY GÜLLÜOĞLU** (see p. 36) to sample Istanbul's finest *baklava*.

WHIRLWIND TOURS

Istanbul for Fun

*Shop for antiques, soak in a steam bath, and
sip cocktails as the sun sets over Europe.*

5 Tünel (see pp. 29, 133)
It's cocktail o'clock every
evening in hip Tünel. For a
spectacular finish to your
tour, head to one of the
neighborhood's rooftop bars.

ÇUKURCUMA

Tünel
Square

Şişhane • ——— Tünel

Whirling **4**
Dervish Hall
(Galata Mevlevihanesi)

Galata Tower **3**
(Galata Kulesi)

Tünel **5**

Haliç •

TERSANE CAD.

Karaköy

GALATA KÖPRÜSÜ

KEMERALTI C.

4 Whirling Dervish Hall
(see pp. 29, 110) Catch
the timeless sight of
Turkey's whirling dervishes.
Retrace your steps to the
Galata Tower or return
to İstiklal Caddesi.

Haliç

ISTANBUL FOR FUN DISTANCE: 3 MILES (5 KM)
TIME: APPROX. 7 HOURS METRO START: TAKSIM

Metro:
Taksim

Galatasaray

② **Galatasaray Hamam**
(Galatasaray Hamamı)

CİHANGİR

① **Cihangir and**
Çukurcuma

YENİ ÇARŞI CAD.

BOĞAZKESEN CAD.

MECLİS-İ MEBUSAN CAD.

Tophane

NECATİBEY CAD.

İstanbul
Boğazi
(Bosporus)

0		400 meters
0		400 Yards

① **Cihangir and Çukurcuma** (see pp. 28, 128–131) Saunter through Istanbul's antiques quarter looking for vintage souvenirs. Make your way to Turnacıbaşı Caddesi.

② **Galatasaray Hamam** (see p. 28) Embrace an age-old Turkish tradition as you indulge yourself in a steam bath. Walk south on İstiklal Caddesi, then Galip Dede Caddesi.

③ **Galata Tower** (see pp. 28–29, 110–111) Enjoy the skyline view from the top of Galata's landmark tower. Continue south on Galip Dede Caddesi.

WHIRLWIND TOURS

Cihangir and Çukurcuma

1 The charming backstreets of Beyoğlu are alive with pavement cafés and offbeat boutiques. You'll find everything here from edgy record stores to dusty antiques outlets. Rummage with the locals at **Cihangir Antik** *(Ağahamam Caddesi 7–8, tel 0212 251 6278)* or try **Ayşe Orberk** *(Turnacıbaşı Sokak 51, tel 0212 252 6635)* for ceramics, lamps, and tea sets.

Akarsu Caddesi & Sıraselviler Caddesi • Metro: Taksim

Browsing tastefully arranged antiques at Ayşe Orberk in Çukurcuma

Galatasaray Hamam

2 Treat yourself to a traditional Turkish steam bath at the Galatasaray Hamam (Galatasaray Hamamı), in business since 1481. After changing into your hamam towel *(peştemal)* and wooden pattens *(takunya),* tiptoe into the ornate marble communal bathing area with its towering dome. Opt for the pasha service: After relaxing on the hamam's heated marble slab for 20 minutes, you'll receive a vigorous soapy massage followed by a bubble bath, a cold shower if you fancy it, and a second massage—this time with warming, aromatic oils.

Turnacıbaşı Caddesi 24 • tel 0212 252 4242 • $$$$ • Nostalgic Tram: Galatasaray • galatasarayhamami.com

Galata Tower

3 A trip up to the top of Istanbul's Galata Tower (Galata Kulesi) is a must for first-time visitors. Many people visit at sunset, so plan to come in the afternoon instead. On reaching the top, you'll be rewarded with staggering views of the entire city. Edge around the tower's wraparound balcony to see **Topkapı Palace** (Topkapı Sarayı; see pp. 62–65) and **Haghia Sophia** (Ayasofya Müzesi; see pp. 60–61) in nearby Sultanahmet, both Bosporus bridges, and the ferries docking at Asian ports in the distance.

Büyük Hendek Sokak 2 · tel 0212 293 8180 · $$$ · Nostalgic Tram: Tünel; Tram: Karaköy

Whirling Dervish Hall

4 No sight embodies old Istanbul like the whirling dervishes, who perform at the Whirling Dervish Hall (Galata Mevlevihanesi; *Sun., 5 p.m.*). Watch as the white-robed dancers spin themselves into a state of religious ecstasy. You can buy tickets at the complex's gate each Sunday morning (see box, p. 110). On nondance days wander into the adjoining museum (*$*) to discover other Mevlevi forms of devotion.

Galip Dede Caddesi 15 · tel 0212 245 4141 · Closed Mon. · $ · Nostalgic Tram: Tünel · galatamevlevihanesimuzesi.gov.tr

Tünel

5 What better way to finish your fun tour than at a rooftop bar in Tünel with a relaxing *rakı* cocktail? For spectacular views while sipping, ride the elevator up to the top-floor bar at the **Anemon Hotel** (*Büyük Hendek Caddesi 11, tel 0212 293 2343, anemonhotels.com*) right next to the Galata Tower (Galata Kulesi). Or walk a little farther to the **Duble Meze Bar** (*Meşrutiyet Caddesi 85, tel 0212 249 5151, dublemezebar.com*) on the top floor of the Palazzo Donizetti Hotel. Order a glass of Turkish Chardonnay—highly rated producers include Sarafin and Corvus.

Intersection of İstiklal Caddesi and Galip Dede Caddesi · Metro: Şişhane/Tünel

GOOD **EATS**

■ **FIRUZ CAFÉ**
A hit with the locals, Firuz serves generous breakfasts and lunches at reasonable prices. The café has a perfect laid-back Çukurcuma vibe. **Defterdar Yokuşu 45–59, tel 0212 252 0241, $$**

■ **GALATA HOUSE**
This quirky restaurant serves traditional Georgian dishes in a building that once served as a jail. Try the *ostri*—veal goulash with paprika, tomato, and cilantro. **Galata Kulesi Sokak 15, tel 0212 2451 861, $$**

■ **GÜNEY RESTAURANT**
This restaurant opposite the Galata Tower serves simple Turkish mezes and kebab dishes. Grab a table outside, on the square overlooking the tower. **Kuledibi Şah Kapısı 2B, tel 0212 249 0393, $$**

Istanbul for History Lovers

Tour the city's more offbeat historical sights for ancient columns, underground reservoirs, and rare archaeological collections.

WHIRLWIND TOURS

5 Little Hagia Sophia Mosque (see p. 33) Admire this finely decorated mosque—once the Church of Saints Sergius and Bacchus. Retrace your steps uphill to Sultanahmet. Ride the tram (T1) four stops west to Aksaray, then walk north on Atatürk Bulvarı.

6 Aqueduct of Valens (Bozdoğan Kemeri)

ŞEHZADEBAŞI CAD

Veznecile

4 Cistern of Philoxenos (see p. 33) Enjoy the cool tranquillity of this underground reservoir. Return to Sultanahmet Meydanı and wander downhill on Su Terazisi Sokak, toward the water.

6 Aqueduct of Valens (see p. 33) You can't miss the massive monument that once funneled water from 155 miles (250 km) of channels into ancient Sultanahmet. Catch a bus or taxi heading north on Atatürk Bulvarı to the Golden Horn.

**ISTANBUL FOR HISTORY LOVERS   DISTANCE: 3.75 MILES (6 KM)
TIME: APPROX. 7 HOURS   TRAM START: SULTANAHMET**

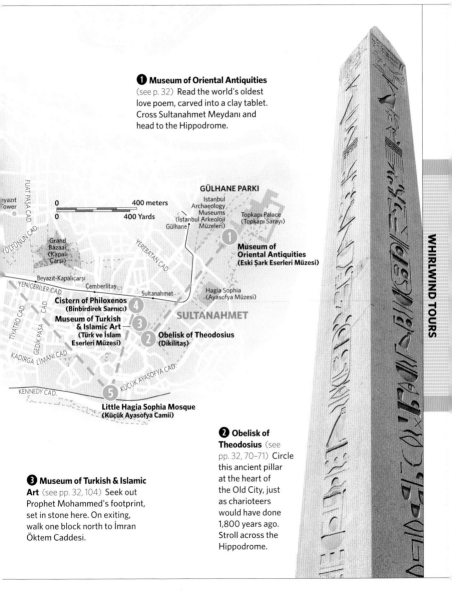

1 **Museum of Oriental Antiquities**
(see p. 32) Read the world's oldest
love poem, carved into a clay tablet.
Cross Sultanahmet Meydanı and
head to the Hippodrome.

GÜLHANE PARKI

İstanbul
Archaeology
Museums
(İstanbul Arkeoloji
Müzeleri)

Topkapı Palace
(Topkapı Sarayı)

Gülhane

Museum of
Oriental Antiquities
(Eski Şark Eserleri Müzesi)

0   400 meters
0   400 Yards

FUAT PAŞA CAD.
eyazıt
ower

PÜLFÜNUN CAD.

Grand
Bazaar
(Kapalı
Çarşı)

YEREBATAN CAD.

Beyazıt-Kapalıçarşı

YENİÇERİLER CAD.

Çemberlitaş
Sultanahmet

Hagia Sophia
(Ayasofya Müzesi)

Cistern of Philoxenos
(Binbirdirek Sarnıcı) **4**

Museum of Turkish
& Islamic Art
(Türk ve İslam
Eserleri Müzesi)

3

TIYATRO CAD.

GEDİK PAŞA CAD.

KADIRGA LİMANI CAD.

SULTANAHMET

2 **Obelisk of Theodosius**
(Dikilitaş)

KÜÇÜK AYASOFYA CAD.

KENNEDY CAD.

5

Little Hagia Sophia Mosque
(Küçük Ayasofya Camii)

3 **Museum of Turkish & Islamic**
Art (see pp. 32, 104) Seek out
Prophet Mohammed's footprint,
set in stone here. On exiting,
walk one block north to İmran
Öktem Caddesi.

2 **Obelisk of**
Theodosius (see
pp. 32, 70–71) Circle
this ancient pillar
at the heart of
the Old City, just
as charioteers
would have done
1,800 years ago.
Stroll across the
Hippodrome.

Museum of Oriental Antiquities

1 One of three collections that comprise the **Istanbul Archaeology Museums** (İstanbul Arkeoloji Müzeleri; see pp. 58–59), the Museum of Oriental Antiquities (Eski Şark Eserleri Müzesi) houses four major collections of pre-Roman exhibits. Highlights include the **Treaty of Kadesh,** the 13th-century declaration of peace between the Hittites and the Egyptians.

Osman Hamdi Bey Yokuşu Sokak • tel 0212 520 7740 • Closed Mon. • $$ • Tram: Gülhane • istanbularkeoloji.gov.tr

Obelisk of Theodosius

2 Of the spoils of war that filled Sultanahmet Meydanı's ancient **Hippodrome** (see p. 70), the Obelisk of Theodosius (Dikilitaş) is the most striking. Some 3,500 years old and 63 feet (19 m) tall, it was shipped to Istanbul in the fourth century. Notice the hieroglyphics—they celebrate ancient Egyptain pharaoh Thutmose III's victory on the banks of the Euphrates River back in 1450 B.C.

Sultanahmet Meydanı • Tram: Sultanahmet

A 17th-century Ottoman geography box at the Museum of Turkish & Islamic Art

Museum of Turkish & Islamic Art

3 Housed in a former Ottoman palace, the Museum of Turkish & Islamic Art (Türk ve İslam Eserleri Müzesi) has a millennium of Islamic artifacts on display. Arranged chronologically, the exhibits take you on a journey back in time. In the first large chamber you'll see elaborate court orders (*firmans*) that carried the sultan's word throughout the land.

Meydanı Sokak 46 • tel 0212 518 1805 • Closed Mon. • $$ • Tram: Sultanahmet

Cistern of Philoxenos

4 Lost for several centuries, the Cistern of Philoxenos (Binbirdirek Sarnıcı) makes a tranquil alternative to the teeming **Basilica Cistern** (Yerebatan Sarnıcı; see pp. 56–57) nearby. The Turkish name for this reservoir translates as "1001 columns." For visitors who wish to count, there are actually 242 50-foot-high (15 m) pillars holding up the vaulted brick ceiling of this ancient water cistern. At the top of many of the pillars you can see personal markings made by the stonemasons.

İmran Öktem Caddesi 4 • tel 0212 518 1001 • $$ • Tram: Sultanahmet • www.binbirdirek.com

Little Hagia Sophia Mosque

5 Like its big sister up the hill, the Little Hagia Sophia Mosque (Küçük Ayasofya Camii) was converted into a mosque after the Ottoman conquest. It, too, glitters with gold leaf. Before you enter, notice the ancient churchlike stonework that makes up the mosque's four walls. The single minaret and ablutions fountain were added after conversion. Step inside and gaze up at the Christian-style nave and cathedral-like half-domes that support the vaulted ceiling.

Küçük Ayasofya Camii Caddesi • tel 0212 227 4480 • Closed Fri. • Tram: Sultanahmet

SAVVY **TRAVELER**

Seeking refreshment at the Aqueduct of Valens? A couple streets northeast, **Vefa Bozacısı** (*Katip Çelebi Caddesi 104, $*), serves two famous fermented drinks: *şıra*, made from grape juice, in the summer; and *boza*, made from millet, in the winter.

Aqueduct of Valens

6 Dozens of bridges once fed water into Istanbul's ancient cisterns. Central to this hydraulic system, the 3,280-foot-long (1,000 m) Aqueduct of Valens (Bozdoğan Kemeri), continued to supply the Ottoman sultans inside the **Topkapı Palace** (Topkapı Sarayı; see pp. 62–65) a millennium later. Wander beneath the arches to get a sense of this structure's sheer scale.

Atatürk Bulvarı • Bus: 41Y, 78, 93

Istanbul for Foodies

Vibrant markets, traditional menus, and sweet treats tantalize the taste buds on this gastronomic tour.

5 Karaköy Fish Market (see p. 37) Admire the fresh sea bass, turbot, and red mullet on market stalls laid out with the catch of the day. Loop northward to Kardeşim Sokak, just south of Tersane Caddesi.

4 Persembe Pazarı (see p. 37) Enjoy the sights, sounds, and smells of Istanbul's hardware district, dotted with unpretentious workers' cafés and teahouses. Walk east on Tersane Caddesi.

Whirling Dervish Hall (Galata Mevlevihanesi)

Tophane

Galata Tower

NECATIBEY CAD

3 Karaköy Güllüoğlu

Karaköy

4 Persembe Pazarı

5 Karaköy Fish Market (Karaköy Balık Pazarı)

TERSANE CAD

Karaköy

6 Rooftop Restaurant

ALATA KÖPRÜSÜ

Haliç

6 Rooftop Restaurant (see p. 37) Enjoy the stunning panoramas of Topkapı Palace, the Blue Mosque, and the Bosporus as you dine on dishes of fresh local fish.

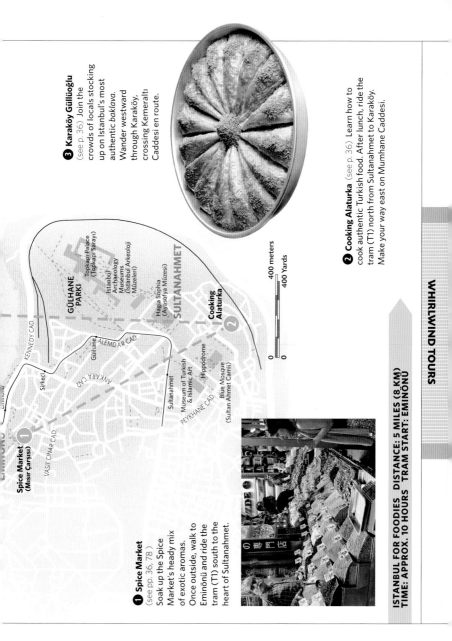

3 Karaköy Güllüoğlu
(see p. 36) Join the crowds of locals stocking up on Istanbul's most authentic *baklava*. Wander westward through Karaköy, crossing Kemeraltı Caddesi en route.

Topkapı Palace
(Topkapı Sarayı)

GÜLHANE PARKI

Istanbul
Archaeology
Museums
(İstanbul Arkeoloji
Müzeleri)

KENNEDY CAD.

Sirkeci

VASIF ÇINAR CAD.

Gülhane

ALEMDAR CAD.

ANKARA CAD.

Hagia Sophia
(Ayasofya Müzesi)

SULTANAHMET

Cooking
Alaturka
2

Sultanahmet

Museum of Turkish
& Islamic Art

PEYKHANE CAD.

Hippodrome

Blue Mosque
(Sultan Ahmet Camii)

0   400 meters
0   400 Yards

EMINÖNÜ

1 Spice Market
(see pp. 36, 78)
Soak up the Spice Market's heady mix of exotic aromas. Once outside, walk to Eminönü and ride the tram (T1) south to the heart of Sultanahmet.

2 Cooking Alaturka (see p. 36) Learn how to cook authentic Turkish food. After lunch, ride the tram (T1) north from Sultanahmet to Karaköy. Make your way east on Mumhane Caddesi.

WHIRLWIND TOURS

ISTANBUL FOR FOODIES DISTANCE: 5 MILES (8 KM)
TIME: APPROX. 10 HOURS TRAM START: EMİNÖNÜ

Spice Market

1 Join the early morning crowd at the Spice Market (Mısır Çarşısı) and treat yourself to some foodie souvenirs. Select a couple of favorite dried fruits and some loose apple tea and have them vacuum-packed for travel. Don't leave without purchasing some Turkish delight *(lokum)*: **Hayat** *(Mısır Çarşısı 8, tel 0212 528 4586)* sells a homemade version sweetened with grape juice and honey.

Entrances on Ragıp Gümüşpala Caddesi, Tahmis Sokak, Çiçek Pazarı Sokak, and Yeni Cami Caddesi • Tram: Eminönü

Cooking Alaturka

2 Cooking Alaturka offers two-hour cooking classes followed by a five-course lunch *(10:30 a.m–2:30 p.m.)* Typical menus might include red lentil and bulgur soup *(ezogelin çorbası)*, zucchini and white cheese fritters *(kabak mücveri)*, and lamb-stuffed eggplant *(karnıyarık)*. Evening sessions are also available *(4:30 p.m.–8:30 p.m.)*.

Akbıyık Caddesi 72A • tel 0212 458 5919 • Closed Sun. • $$$$ • Tram: Sultanahmet • cookingalaturka.com

Getting to grips with lamb-stuffed eggplant at Cooking Alaturka

Karaköy Güllüoğlu

3 *Baklava* specialist Karaköy Güllüoğlu has been a place of pilgrimage for the sweet-toothed since it opened in 1949. The varieties of this filo-pastry-and-nut treat range from milky *nuriye*, with walnuts and a creamy sauce, to pistachio Palace Wraps. Savor a selection with a cup of Turkish coffee in the café area, and don't forget to take some home.

Mumhane Caddesi 171 • tel 0212 249 9680 • $ • Tram: Karaköy • karakoygulluoglu.com

Perşembe Pazarı

4 Skimming the northern shores of the Golden Horn, Perşembe Pazarı is the city's colorful hardware district. Its meandering alleyways are dotted with ancient Ottoman trading houses (*hans*) and industrial shops. The neighborhood is also scattered with excellent locals-only eateries and street-food vendors. Stroll along the waterfront, then stop at one of Perşembe Pazarı's low-key garden cafés for a tulip-shaped glass of Turkish tea.

Tersane Caddesi and around • Tram: Karaköy

SAVVY **TRAVELER**

If this Whirlwind Tour only serves to whet your appetite, book a culinary walk with local outfit **Culinary Backstreets** (*$$$$, culinarybackstreets.com*). Seven different walks wind their way across Istanbul, dropping in to Ottoman-era bakeries and traditional pickle-makers, then sampling savory kebabs and regional desserts en route. Walks last between three and six hours, and are limited to a maximum of ten participants.

Karaköy Fish Market

5 Nestled behind one of the neighborhood's hectic ferry terminals, Karaköy Fish Market (Karaköy Balık Pazarı) is one of Istanbul's most vibrant fish and seafood markets. Stallholders sell everything from anchovies and mackerel to red mullet and turbot, depending on the season. Kiosks are interspersed with crowded restaurants serving up simple, grilled and fried fish dishes.

Northwest corner of Galata Köprüsü • Tram: Karaköy

Rooftop Restaurant

6 Round off your day with a meal at one of Karaköy's superb fish restaurants. A local landmark since it opened in 1923, Tarihi Karaköy Balıkçısı began life as a humble seafood eatery. Over the intervening decades, the menu has remained refreshingly simple, featuring dishes like chunky fish stew and sea bass in parchment. However, today, patrons may also dine in Tarihi Karaköy Grifin, the establishment's panoramic rooftop room.

Tersane Caddesi, Kardeşim Sokak 45 • tel 0212 243 4080 • $$$ • Tram: Karaköy • tarihikarakoybalikcisi.com

Istanbul in a Weekend with Kids

*From climbing Byzantine towers to rumbling along on a
historic tram, this tour will enchant kids of all ages.*

❶ Miniatürk (see p. 40) See Turkey's major
tourist sites in miniature. Head to İmrahor
Caddesi and jump aboard any bus heading
south. Alight at Kırmızı Minare.

❷ Rahmi M. Koç Museum (see p. 40) Tour
the halls of vintage cars. Take the bus (36T
or 54HT) to Taksim Square. Walk north on
Cumhuriyet Caddesi.

❸ Military Museum (see p. 41)
Watch the Mehter Band at the
Military Museum. Backtrack
along Cumhuriyet Caddesi
to Taksim Square, then stroll
southwest along pedestrianized
İstiklal Caddesi.

**WEEKEND WITH KIDS DAY 1   DISTANCE: 6.5 MILES (10.5 KM)
TIME: APPROX. 8 HOURS   START: MINIATÜRK**

WHIRLWIND TOURS

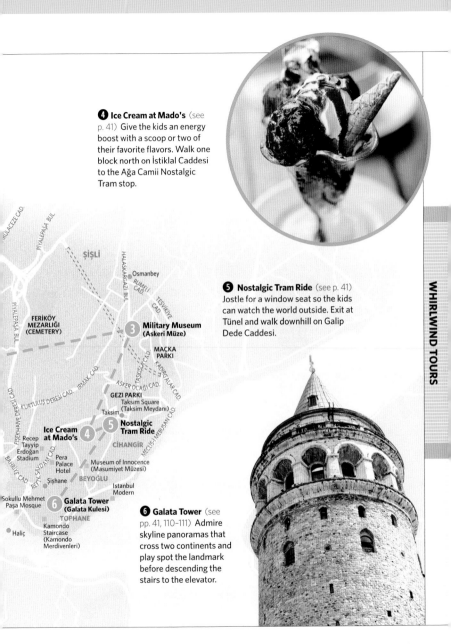

4 **Ice Cream at Mado's** (see p. 41) Give the kids an energy boost with a scoop or two of their favorite flavors. Walk one block north on İstiklal Caddesi to the Ağa Camii Nostalgic Tram stop.

5 **Nostalgic Tram Ride** (see p. 41) Jostle for a window seat so the kids can watch the world outside. Exit at Tünel and walk downhill on Galip Dede Caddesi.

6 **Galata Tower** (see pp. 41, 110–111) Admire skyline panoramas that cross two continents and play spot the landmark before descending the stairs to the elevator.

Map labels:

MÜLACEZE CAD.
PIYALEPAŞA BUL.
ŞİŞLİ
HALASKARGAZI BUL.
Osmanbey
RUMELI CAD.
TEŞVİKİYE CAD.
PIYALEPAŞA BUL.
FERİKÖY MEZARLIĞI (CEMETERY)
BAHRİYE CAD.
KURTULUŞ DERESİ CAD.
FİŞEKHANE DERESİ CAD.
IRMAK CAD.
3 **Military Museum (Askeri Müze)**
MAÇKA PARKI
TAŞKIŞLA CAD.
ASKER OCAĞI CAD.
KADIRGALAR CAD.
GEZİ PARKI
Taksim Square (Taksim Meydanı)
Taksim
MECLISİ MEBUSAN CAD.
Ice Cream at Mado's **4**
5 **Nostalgic Tram Ride**
Recep Tayyip Erdoğan Stadium
REFİK SAYDAM CAD.
CİHANGİR
Pera Palace Hotel
Şişhane
Museum of Innocence (Masumiyet Müzesi)
BEYOĞLU
İstanbul Modern
Sokullu Mehmet Paşa Mosque
6 **Galata Tower (Galata Kulesi)**
TOPHANE
Haliç
Kamondo Staircase (Kamondo Merdivenleri)

Istanbul's Blue Mosque in miniature at the Miniatürk theme park

Miniatürk

1 Miniatürk re-creates more than 100 of Turkey's major landmarks, including the **Galata Tower** (Galata Kulesi; see opposite), at which your day's tour will end. Young kids love riding the train that chugs its way through the park.

İmrahor Caddesi • tel 0212 222 2882 • $$ • Bus: 36T, 41ST, 47, or 54HT

Rahmi M. Koç Museum

2 This vast transportation museum showcases antique toys, model ships, and an immense collection of vintage cars, among other things. Its location at the former Hasköy Dockyards on the northern banks of the Golden Horn is particularly well suited for its star attraction, the U.S.-built Turkish submarine TCG *Uluçalireis (seen via guided tour, $).* Other highlights include a Douglas DC-3 Dakota airplane, suspended outdoors and accessible via a set of steep stairs.

Hasköy Caddesi 5 • tel 0212 369 6600 • Closed Mon., Jan 1., and Dec. 31 • $$ • Bus: 36T, 47, 47E, 47C, 47N, 54HT, or 54HS • rmk-museum.org.tr

Military Museum

3 From jewel-encrusted swords to ancient armor, the Military Museum (Askeri Müze) has it all. If the timing works, your kids will love having an archery lesson *(Wed. and Sat., 2 p.m. and 3 p.m.)* in the Cannon Exhibition Hall.

Cumhuriyet Caddesi • tel 0212 233 2720 • Closed Mon. and Tues. • $ • Metro: Osmanbey • askerimuze.tsk.tr

SAVVY **TRAVELER**

Time your trip to see the world's oldest military ensemble, the **Mehter band,** performing outside the Military Museum *(3 p.m. and 4 p.m. daily, Wed.–Sun.).* In Ottoman times, cymbal-smashing Mehter bands were famed for the slow victory songs they played while marching through conquered towns.

Ice Cream at Mado's

4 In warm weather ice-cream vendors are dotted along **İstiklal Caddesi** (see pp. 134–135), often dressed in traditional Ottoman costume. Join the line at the Mado ice-cream café, and treat your kids to an alfresco scoop. Better still, step inside for a sundae.

İstiklal Caddesi 121 • tel 0212 245 4631 • $ • Nostalgic Tram: Ağa Camii

Nostalgic Tram Ride

5 Rattle your way along this mile-long shopping avenue in one of the petite red tramcars that shuttle between **Tünel** (see p. 133) and Taksim. Just hop on with the kids and ride all the way to Tünel. The **İstanbulkart** transit pass (see p. 177) is valid on the Nostalgic Tram, and kids under the age of five travel free.

Five stops: Taksim, Ağa Camii, Galatasaray, Odakule, and Tünel • $

Galata Tower

6 You're more likely to have to wait a little longer to access the Galata Tower (Galata Kulesi) at this time of day, but it is certainly worth it to see the deep red sunset over the Golden Horn. Kids of all ages will find it truly magical.

Büyük Hendek Sokak 2 • tel 0212 293 8180 • $$$ • Nostalgic Tram: Tünel; Tram: Karaköy

Istanbul in a Weekend with Kids

*Highlights of this tour include a high-speed train,
a ferry, and a mansion stuffed with toys.*

Galata Tower
(Galata Kulesi) — Istanbul Modern
TOPHANE

ATATÜRK KÖPRÜSÜ — Kamondo Staircase
Haliç — Kamondo Merdivenleri)
Eminönü 5
Fish Sandwich

GALATA KÖPRÜSÜ

Marmaray Under
the Bosporus 2

Istanbul
Railway Museum
(İstanbul Demiryolu Müzesi) 1

TAHTAKALE **SİRKECİ**

GÜLHANE
PARKI
Topkapı Palace
(Topkapı Sarayı)

Basilica Cistern
(Yerebatan
Sarnıcı) — Hagia Eirene

Hagia Sophia
(Ayasofya Müzesi)

1 Istanbul Railway Museum (see pp. 44, 77) Dip into Sirkeci Train Station for a peek at Turkish rail travel through the ages. Ride one of the escalators to the Marmaray's subterranean station.

2 Marmaray Under the Bosporus (see p. 44) Make the five-minute subterranean train journey to Ayrılık Çeşmesi in Asia. Flag down a taxi to Ömer Paşa Caddesi, 15 minutes to the south.

Marmara Deniz
(Sea of Marmar

3 Istanbul Toy Museum (see p. 45) Tour themed rooms that include a submarine, a room full of dolls, a train carriage, and a police cell. Take a taxi to the Kadıköy pier.

WEEKEND WITH KIDS DAY 2   DISTANCE: 12.5 MILES (20 KM)
TIME: APPROX. 7 HOURS   TRAM START: SIRKECI

5 **Eminönü Fish Sandwich** (see pp. 45, 86) Round off your day with a local tradition—eat a grilled fish sandwich on the waterfront. Dare your kids to try the pickle juice!

aiden's Tower
iz Kulesi)

HAREM SAHIL YOLU

TIBBİYE CAD.

DR. EYÜP AKSOY CAD.

TIBBİYE CAD.

D-100

BEHİÇ BEY CAD.

Ayrılıkçeşme

TAŞKÖPRÜ CAD.

KADIKÖY

Kadıköy Ferry **4**

O-1

Kadıköy
Kadıköy
Fish Market

MODA CAD.

FAHRETTİN KERİM GÖKAY CAD.

Istanbul Toy Museum
(Istanbul Oyuncak Müzesi) **3**

0 ———————— 1 kilometer
0 ———————— 1 mile

4 **Kadıköy Ferry** (see p. 45) Snap photos of your kids against the Old City skyline. Disembark at the Eminönü ferry pier.

Istanbul Railway Museum

1 The compact Istanbul Railway Museum (İstanbul Demiryolu Müzesi) may occupy just one room, but, crammed with more than 300 railway artifacts, it will satisfy even the most ardent of young train buffs. At the center of the museum is a full-sized driver cab with plenty of levers and knobs to look at.

Ankara Caddesi • tel 0212 520 7885 • Closed Sun. and Mon. • Tram: Sirkeci

Marmaray Under the Bosporus

2 Impress your kids with the idea that, in a matter of minutes, they will be transported from one continent to another. The Marmaray rail link zips beneath the Bosporus, allowing passengers to speed from the historic highlights of Sultanahmet in Europe to the seaside promenade of Asian Istanbul in a flash.

Sirkeci Tren Garı • Ankara Caddesi • $ • Tram: Sirkeci; Marmaray: Sirkeci

Soldiers stand guard in front of the Istanbul Toy Museum.

Istanbul Toy Museum

3 Spilling over a traditional Ottoman-style wooden mansion (*yalı*), the Istanbul Toy Museum (İstanbul Oyuncak Müzesi) houses thousands of toys and games from around the world that date from the 1700s to the present day. Vitrines overflow with international treasures, from local 1970s Fatoş stuffed animals to the second floor's stellar outer-space-themed display. The museum has a workshop, in which kids can get their hands dirty with various activities from mosaic-making through puppet-making.

Ömer Paşa Caddesi, Dr. Zeki Zeren Sokak 15 • tel 0216 359 4550 • Closed Mon • $$
• Bus: 10, 14Ç, 14 KS, 17, 19F, GZ1, ER1 • istanbuloyuncakmuzesi.com

IN **THE KNOW**

Traveling with teens as well as little kids? Stop to shop on the way to the Istanbul Toy Museum. The museum sits around a 15-minute walk north of **Bağdat Caddesi.** This leafy 8-mile-long (13 km) avenue is one of the city's premier shopping boulevards.

Kadıköy Ferry

4 For a real sense of the city, nothing beats cruising across the Bosporus by ferry. Open decks mean that families can find a sunny spot, then pick out Istanbul's spellbinding sights, such as the **Blue Mosque** (Sultan Ahmet Camii; see pp. 54–55). Buy the kids a refreshing orange juice from one of the ship's roving waiters.

TurYol Ferries • Kadıköy İskelesi • $ • turyol.com

Eminönü Fish Sandwich

5 Make straight for the wooden, Ottoman-style boats moored up on the shores of the Golden Horn at Eminönü. Operating throughout the day, these boats serve hot fish sandwiches (*balık ekmek*) by the hundreds. Your kids will love the novelty of the chefs frying up the fish and stuffing the sandwiches while the boat rocks back and forth on the waves. See if you can tempt the children to try some bright-colored pickled vegetables (*turşu*) on the side—you can buy them from a kiosk nearby.

Ragıp Gümüşpala Caddesi • $ • Tram: Eminönü

PART 2

Istanbul's Neighborhoods

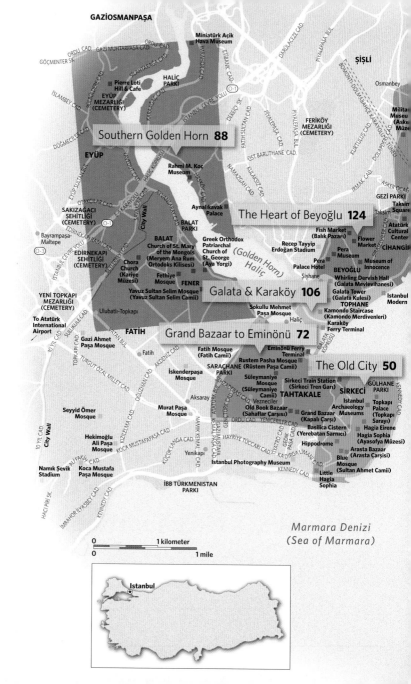

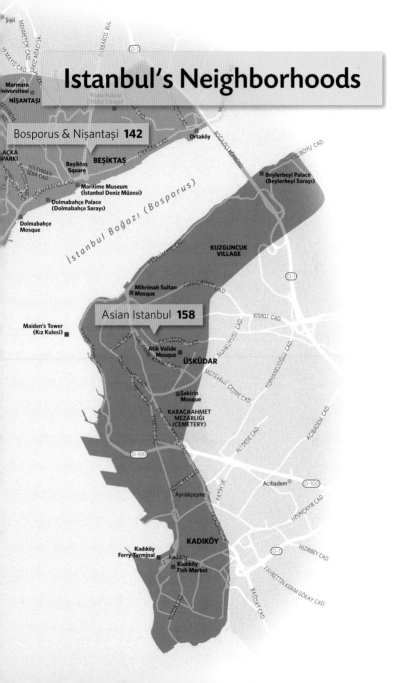

Istanbul's Neighborhoods

Şişli

BARBAROS BUL.

MEHMETÇIK CAD.

19 MAYIS CAD.

KIRTEK AGAÇI SK. HASAT

Marmara
Üniversitesi
NİŞANTAŞI

Yıldız Palace
(Yıldız Sarayı)

ESVIKIYE

KADIRGALAR CAD.

Bosporus & Nişantaşı **142**

Ortaköy

BOĞAZİÇİ KÖPRÜSÜ

YALIBOYU CAD.

AÇKA
PARKI

SÜLEYMAN
SEBA CAD.

Beşiktaş
Square

BEŞİKTAŞ

ÇIRAĞAN CAD.

DOLMABAHÇE CAD.

Maritime Museum
(İstanbul Deniz Müzesi)

Dolmabahçe Palace
(Dolmabahçe Sarayı)

Beylerbeyi Palace
(Beylerbeyi Sarayı)

İstanbul Boğazı (Bosporus)

Dolmabahçe
Mosque

PAŞALIMANI CAD.

KUZGUNCUK
VILLAGE

CUMHURİYET CAD.

O-1

Mihrimah Sultan
Mosque

KISIKLI CAD.

Asian Istanbul **158**

Maiden's Tower
(Kız Kulesi)

ŞEMSIPAŞA CAD.

HALK CAD.

DR. FAHRI ATABEY CAD.

ÇAVUŞDERE CAD.

NUHKUYUSU CAD.

TOPHANELIOĞLU CAD.

Atik Valide
Mosque

ÜSKÜDAR

MÜTEVELLİ ÇEŞME CAD.

TUNUSBAĞI CAD.

TIBBİYE CAD.

Şakirin
Mosque

AÇIBADEM CAD.

KARACAAHMET
MEZARLIĞI
(CEMETERY)

ALİ DEDE CAD.

NÜHI DEDE AYSEL CAD.

D-100

İNÖNÜ CAD.

Acıbadem

D-100

UZUNÇAYIR CAD.

FATİH SK.

Ayrılıkçeşme

HİZIRBEY CAD.

O-1

ADLİYE SK.

KADIKÖY

Kadıköy
Ferry Terminal

Kadıköy

Kadıköy
Fish Market

FAHRETTİN KERİM GÖKAY CAD.

BAĞDAT CAD.

ACIDAÇ CAD.

The Old City

Stand in Sultanahmet Square and take a look around you. Three empires—first Roman, then Byzantine, then Ottoman—ruled much of the known world from this very spot. Emperors, sultans, and caliphs prayed at the Hagia Sophia, worshiped at the Blue Mosque, and enjoyed a life of leisure at Topkapı Palace. Of course, with power comes wealth, and the riches you'll see—golden mosaics, sparkling jewels, and wall-to-wall İznik tiles—are just a fraction of those that once existed. So numerous are the spellbinding sights in this compact neighborhood that some were ignored for centuries. The eerie underground Basilica Cistern and the colorful Great Palace Mosaic are both relatively recent discoveries. To see all of the sights in Sultanahmet in a single day could overwhelm the senses, so be sure to take time out in shady Gülhane Park or find a quiet corner of the Istanbul Archaeology Museums for a moment's contemplation.

○ **A view of the immense,
domed interior of the
Hagia Sophia from its
upper gallery**

The Old City

Istanbul's most significant historic sites cluster tightly together in the city's oldest quarter.

6 Istanbul Archaeology Museums (see pp. 58–59)
View a diverse collection of artifacts from all corners of the vast Ottoman Empire. Exit the park and walk south on Soğukçeşme Sokak.

Haliç (Golden Horn)

5 Gülhane Park (see pp. 57–58) Take a relaxing stroll on the slopes below Topkapı Palace. As you return to the park entrance, don't exit—instead take the uphill path toward the museums.

4 Hagia Sophia (see pp. 60–61) Pause to appreciate the ingenius structure of this Byzantine church, so advanced for its time. Continue north on Alemdar Caddesi.

KENNEDY CAD.

SİRKECİ

HÜDAVENDIGAR CAD.

EBUSSUUD CAD.

Gülhane

ALEMDAR CAD.

HÜKÜMET KONAGI CAD.

5 Gülhane Park
(Gülhane Parkı)

7 Topkapı Palace
(Topkapı Saray)

6 Istanbul Archaeology Museums
(İstanbul Arkeoloji Müzeleri)

7 Topkapı Palace (see pp. 62–65) Pass through the Imperial Gate to see the splendor in which the Ottoman sultans lived for almost 500 years.

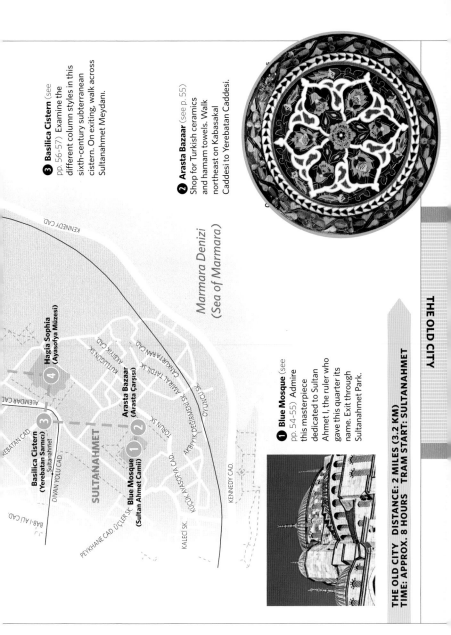

❸ Basilica Cistern (see pp. 56–57) Examine the different column styles in this sixth-century subterranean cistern. On exiting, walk across Sultanahmet Meydani.

❷ Arasta Bazaar (see p. 55) Shop for Turkish ceramics and hamam towels. Walk northeast on Kabasakal Caddesi to Yerebatan Caddesi.

Marmara Denizi
(Sea of Marmara)

KENNEDY CAD.

Hagia Sophia
(Ayasofya Müzesi)
❹

AKBIYIK CAD.

KUTLUGÜN SK.

Basilica Cistern
(Yerebatan Sarnıcı)
Sultanahmet
❸

ALEMDAR CAD.

YEREBATAN CAD.

DİVAN YOLU CAD.

BAB-I ALİ CAD.

SULTANAHMET

Arasta Bazaar
(Arasta Çarşısı)
❷

Blue Mosque
(Sultan Ahmet Camii)
❶

AMİRAL TAFDİL SK.

ÇAMURTI TRAM CAD.

TORUN SK.

OYUNCU SK.

AKBIYIK DEĞİRMENİ SK.

KÜÇÜK AYASOFYA CAD.

PEYKHANE CAD. ÜÇLER SK.

KALECİ SK.

KENNEDY CAD.

❶ Blue Mosque (see pp. 54–55) Admire this masterpiece dedicated to Sultan Ahmet I, the ruler who gave this quarter its name. Exit through Sultanahmet Park.

**THE OLD CITY DISTANCE: 2 MILES (3.2 KM)
TIME: APPROX. 8 HOURS TRAM START: SULTANAHMET**

Blue Mosque

Among the Old City's most recognizable sights, the Blue Mosque (Sultan Ahmet Camii) was the last great mosque to be built in Istanbul. Combining Byzantine and Islamic architectural styles, its dimensions are immense—it's large enough to accommodate 10,000 people—and the structure is perfectly symmetrical. On arrival, see how the domes cascade down to the ground, flanked on either side by three minarets. It is said that, when Sultan Ahmet I commissioned the building in 1606, he asked for his temple to have gold *(altın)*, not six *(altı)*, minarets. Either way, this mosque has more prayer towers than any other mosque in the city.

Once inside, the eye is drawn to the upper galleries, ringed with the 20,000 blue İznik tiles (see p. 79) from which the mosque takes its unofficial name—it should be Sultan Ahmet Mosque. Above the galleries sits the great dome and the succession of semidomes that you see from outside, all supported on four stout, fluted columns.

Light streams into the Blue Mosque through an impressive number of windows; there are 260 in all.

Each dome is hand-painted with elaborate geometric frescoes and verses from the Koran. Immediately facing the main entrance, you'll see the white marble pulpit (minbar), visible from every position in the mosque. The Imam delivers his Friday sermon from here. If no one is at prayer, feel free to wander discretely toward the pulpit to examine its fine, carved decoration. Beside the pulpit is the mihrab, the niche that marks the direction of Mecca.

IN **THE KNOW**

Istanbul's mosques are working mosques, which means they close for prayer. The call to prayer sounds five times a day: two hours before dawn; dawn; midday; mid-afternoon; and sunset. Each mosque may be closed for up to 90 minutes during this time.

Sultanahmet Meydanı • Closed Fri. a.m. and during prayer times • $ (Donation) • Tram: Sultanahmet

Arasta Bazaar

2

The Arasta Bazaar (Arasta Çarşısı) is a smaller, laid-back version of the **Grand Bazaar** (Kapalı Çarşı; see pp. 80–83) and offers a welcome alfresco break between visits to the **Blue Mosque** and the **Basilica Cistern** (Yerebatan Sarnıcı; see pp. 56–57). You may be invited to drink a glass of tea (çay) as you window-shop, but you won't be hassled. If you do intend to buy, there is everything from carpets to gold necklaces and hand-painted ceramics from the city of Kütahya (an important producer since the Ottoman era). The carpet emporium **Mehmet Çetinkaya Gallery** (Tavukhane Sokak 7, tel 0212 517 6808) is popular with locals. The rent from these 90 or so stalls once used to pay the upkeep of the Blue Mosque. As you meander through, look for the occasional intact floor mosaic and some curiously old pillars and columns. The market was built on top of Byzantine Emperor Justinian's sixth-century palace. Today, you can see more of what once formed a huge mosaic pavement at the **Great Palace Mosaic Museum** (Büyük Saray Mozaikleri Müzesi; see p. 71), situated beneath the bazaar.

Arasta Çarşısı • tel 0212 516 0733 • Closed Sun. • Tram: Sultanahmet • arastabazaar.com

THE OLD CITY

One of two huge blocks carved with the face of Medusa, now used as a pedestal at the cistern

Basilica Cistern

Descend the rickety wooden staircase to the Basilica Cistern (Yerebatan Sarnıcı) and feast your eyes on one of the most arresting sights in downtown Istanbul: an underground reservoir measuring 105,000 square feet (9,755 sq m) and supported on 336 stone columns. Until the 1980s, visitors rowed through the spooky darkness by boat—there is a scene in the movie *From Russia with Love*, in which James Bond (Sean Connery) does just that. Today, you can tour the cistern on foot, via raised wooden walkways that weave between the pillars.

The glow from red and orange lamps and the trancelike Turkish music contribute to the eerie atmosphere. Run your fingers over the finely detailed columns that you pass. Many of these 30-foot-tall (9 m) pillars propping up the vaulted ceiling were pilfered from ancient Roman ruins. Seek out the **Hen's Eye column.** Its tearlike indentations supposedly represent the efforts of the 7,000 slaves whose blood, sweat, and sobs built the cisterns during the sixth century. Look up and you'll see that most columns are crested with roll-topped Ionic capitals or elaborate Corinthian capitals. At the western edge of the cistern, the wooden pathway leads the way to two carved heads of Medusa. So rich was the Byzantine stonework aboveground, that locals thought nothing of using these magnificent sculptured heads as mere pedestals.

Yerebatan Caddesi 1–3 • tel 0212 512 1570 • $ • Tram: Sultanahmet • yerebatansarnici.com

Hagia Sophia

4 See pp. 60–61.

Ayasofya Meydanı • tel 0212 522 1750 • Closed Mon. • $$$ • Tram: Sultanahmet • ayasofyamuzesi.gov.tr

Gülhane Park

5 Originally, Gülhane Park (Gülhane Parkı) formed part of the **Topkapı Palace** (Topkapı Sarayı; see pp. 62–65) gardens. The Ottoman sultans built it for the use of harem girls and A-list visitors. Today you, too, can saunter through its acres of flowers and leafy shade trees.

A central path leads through a grove of soaring Mediterranean plane trees to the **Column of the Goths.** The Latin inscription on the base of this 61-foot-tall (18.6 m) pillar commemorates a Roman victory over the heathen Goths who once threatened the city. Place your hands on the column if you like—you could well be touching the oldest Roman monument in the entire city.

Follow any one of several paths for a steady climb to the park's northeastern perimeter. Depending on the timing of your visit, the borders of the path will be packed with

GOOD **EATS**

■ **ALBURA KATHISMA**
A classic Sultanahmet eatery that has been dishing up İskender kebabs from the Bursa region and Turkish flatbread (pide) pizza from the Black Sea for decades. **Akbıyık Caddesi 26, tel 0212 517 9031, $**

■ **BALIKÇI SABAHATTIN**
This popular fish restaurant is situated in a crumbling mansion house with a leafy dining terrace and serves exceptional seafood dishes. **Şehit Hasan Kuyu Sokak 51, tel 0212 458 1824, $$$**

■ **TARIHI SULTANAHMET KÖFTECISI**
This hugely popular restaurant has the simplest menu: grilled meatballs (köfte), bean salad, soup, and a sweet semolina dessert. **Divan Yolu Caddesi 12, tel 0212 520 0566, $**

flowers—swathes of tiny grape hyacinths and tulips in spring and fragrant roses all through summer. Indeed, *gülhane* translates as "house of roses," and sultans once spent their days lounging alongside these flowerbeds. If you're feeling thirsty, be sure to make a final stop at the **Gülhane Park Café** (see p. 156), perched on the topmost edge of the park overlooking the spot at which the Bosporus meets the Golden Horn. Young couples have used this romantic location for courting since the gardens opened a century ago.

Alemdar Caddesi • Tram: Gülhane

Istanbul Archaeology Museums

6 The Istanbul Archaeology Museums (İstanbul Arkeoloji Müzeleri) combine three sights in one. For the purposes of this tour, the focus is on the **Museum of Archaeology** (Arkeoloji Müzesi), although all three museums are worth visiting if you have time. Located on the eastern side of the complex as you pass through the main entrance, the Museum of Archaeology houses artifacts representing major periods in Turkish history. The first floor focuses on the ancient Aegean cities of Ephesus, Miletus, and Aphrodisias. In particular, the galleries focus on statuary from ancient sites, including the Temple of Zeus at Pergamum. Also among the exhibits are a number of sarcophagi (ancient stone burial tombs). They include the Sidamara Sarcophagus and, in Gallery 8, the remarkable **Alexander Sarcophagus.** Once thought to belong to Alexander the Great, this showpiece is finely decorated with battles between Persians and Greeks on one side and horseback hunting scenes on another. The ground floor is also home to a

SAVVY **TRAVELER**

With combined collections that amount to more than one million objects in total, the Istanbul Archaelogical Museums complex constitutes a major site in its own right. You're unlikely to have time for all three, so opt for just one and return to see the others on another day. If the **Museum of Archaeology** (Arkeoloji Müzesi) doesn't appeal, head instead to the **Museum of Oriental Antiquities** (Eski Şark Eserleri Müzesi; see p. 32) or the **Tile Pavilion** (Çinili Köşk Müzesi; see p. 105).

The Sidamara Sarcophagus is intricately carved with friezes.

Children's Museum, which features a full-scale model of the Trojan Horse. On the second floor of the museum, exhibits from Lebanon, Palestine, and Cyprus reflect how far the Ottoman Empire's tentacles once stretched. Here, you'll see the bronze snake head from the **Serpentine Column** (see p. 21) in the Hippodrome. In Gallery 1, on the third floor, an entire burial tomb from a merchant family in Palmyra in Syria is worth seeking out. Head to the fourth floor to see the eighth-century B.C. Siloam inscription, one of the world's oldest surviving Hebrew texts.

Osman Hamdi Bey Yokuşu Sokak • tel 0212 520 7740 • Closed Mon. • $$ • Tram: Gülhane • istanbularkeoloji.gov.tr

Topkapı Palace

7 See pp. 62–65.

Bab-ı Hümayun Caddesi • tel 0212 512 0480 • Closed Tues. • $$$ (harem, an additional $$) • Tram: Gülhane • topkapisarayi.gov.tr

Hagia Sophia

This jewel of Byzantine architecture was the world's largest cathedral for a thousand years.

Despite damage to its bottom half, the Deësis mosaic remains one of Hagia Sophia's finest.

As you approach the Hagia Sophia (Ayasofya Müzesi) from Sultanahmet Meydanı, pause to take in the building's unique profile. It was built by Emperor Justinian in A.D. 537 as a Christian cathedral. After conquering Constantinople in 1453 (see pp. 66–69), Sultan Mehmet II converted the handsome church into a mosque—note the addition of the four minarets. In 1935, under the direction of Turkey's first president, Mustafa Kemal Atatürk, the building was restored and opened to the public as a museum.

THE OLD CITY

■ Breathtaking Interior

Start your visit by stepping into the Hagia Sophia's narthex (lobby). As you pass through this lofty vestibule, look up to the ceiling to see a mosaic of Emperor Leo VI bowing down before Christ Pantocrator. Then walk on into the vast main chamber and prepare to be amazed. Some 120 feet (56 m) above your head, the golden dome rests on 40 arched windows. Many visitors try in vain to capture the scene on a smartphone, but it is far better simply to lose yourself in this light-filled spectacle instead.

■ The Influence of Islam

The Hagia Sophia served as a mosque for almost 500 years, and vestiges of its Islamic past are all around you. Walk over to the marble pulpit (minbar) in the building's northern arcade and note the huge pendant chandelier—similar to those found in the city's mosques—hanging above. Scan the horseshoe-shaped **Upper Gallery** to see eight enormous green medallions (levhas) inscribed with the names of Allah, the prophet Mohammed, the first four caliphs, and Mohammed's two eldest grandsons.

IN **THE KNOW**

In the northwest corner of the Hagia Sophia's main chamber stands the white **Wishing Column.** The base of this rectangular marble column is encased in bronze, and in the casing is a circular window that reveals a small hole. They say that if you pop your thumb inside the hole and make a wish as you rotate it once, clockwise, your wish will come true.

■ A Mosaic Tour

Make your way upstairs, where a circular green stone marks the spot on which the throne of the Byzantine empresses once stood, providing the best panorama in the house.

Walk on to the **South Gallery,** where a number of pre-Ottoman mosaics shimmer in the subdued light. The first is the incomplete **Deësis mosaic,** which shows the Virgin Mary and John the Baptist asking Christ for forgiveness on behalf of humanity. The **Empress Zoe mosaic** shows Christ Pantocrator, flanked by Byzantine Emperor Constantine IX and his beautiful wife, and the **Comnenus mosaic** depicts the Virgin and Child with Emperor John II and Empress Irene alongside them.

Ayasofya Meydanı • tel 0212 522 1750 • Closed Mon. • $$$ • Tram: Sultanahmet • ayasofyamuzesi.gov.tr

Topkapı Palace

Sumptuous living quarters and jewel-encrusted treasures betray the extraordinary wealth of the Ottoman dynasty.

The Hall of the Ablution Fountain is just one of many rooms decorated with intricate İznik designs.

Sultan Mehmet II started building the Topkapı Palace (Topkapı Sarayı) in 1459. To grasp the enormity of this royal residence, after buying your ticket, survey two scale models located just inside the Gate of Salutation. The first shows the position of the palace and its grounds on Seraglio Point, the second details the Second, Third, and Fourth Courtyards. As you tour the buildings, you'll see treasures from Morocco to Iraq, Crimea to Serbia—all shipped from the four corners of the Ottoman Empire and now on display inside.

Royal Entrance

As you pass through the imposing **Imperial Gate** on Sultanahmet Meydanı, look above it to see a finely gilded inscription. The sultan's name is inscribed in Arabic on the top line. On entering the **First Courtyard,** notice how thick and high the walls are—this sturdy perimeter was built to defend the royal family from intruders.

Revel in your first taste of imperial splendor as you walk directly through the sultan's private parkland toward the ticket office. A vast Bosporus view opens up on your right. On your left is the **Imperial Mint** *(closed to the public)* in which many tons of Ottoman gold were once counted. Court visitors would smarten themselves up before the finely styled iron doors of the **Gate of Salutation** through which you'll now pass. Today, all visitors must head through a body scanner before entering the **Second Courtyard.**

Private View

There was a time when only visiting foreigners, Ottoman VIPs, and the sultan's private army of Janissary guards could see the sight before your eyes. The palace kitchens are on your right—notice the colossal chimneys rising up from the roof. The harem lies to your left. Peacocks, tortoises, and exotic animals once roamed freely in this serene walled garden.

SAVVY **TRAVELER**

Entry to the **harem** incurs an additional fee *($$)*. Buy a ticket on arrival—there's a kiosk in front of the harem entrance—and visit some of the palace's other sights while awaiting your designated time slot. Note when the ticket office closes *(4 p.m. in winter and 6 p.m. in summer)*. Alternatively, buy a **Museum Pass İstanbul** (see pp. 177–178) in advance, which covers entry to all sights at Topkapı Palace, including the harem.

The Sultan's Kitchen

Enter the palace kitchens, once a busy hub providing for 5,000 staff members. If you're wondering why there is so much Chinese and Japanese porcelain in the antechambers, it is because the Ottomans believed that the dye used in its production neutralized poison. This is nonsense, of course, but such rumors kept fine china coming down the Silk Road from Beijing.

Inside the Harem

On the opposite side of the courtyard, purchase a ticket to visit the harem if you have not already done so. The name translates as "forbidden," and any man caught walking through its İznik-tiled entranceway to see the

The lavish Carriage Gate in the Second Courtyard marks the entrance to the harem at Topkapı Palace.

sultan's concubines might once have paid with his life. Follow the **Golden Road,** a tile-lined path that connects the key chambers, to the sumptuous **Apartments of the Queen Mother,** where you can view her divan and intricate private baths.

■ THIRD COURTYARD
Walk through the **Gate of Felicity** into the **Third Courtyard,** the private domain of the sultan. Let's not forget that the Ottoman rulers were once

among the world's richest men, so brace yourself for some serious glitz. First walk straight into the **Chamber of Petitions** directly ahead, where the sultan received audiences. Government officials discussed matters of state with the sultan as he sat on his emerald-encrusted throne. This courtyard also served as an imperial pleasure area, complete with the whitewashed **Enderûn Library** and the porticoed **Conqueror's Kiosk.**

■ JEWELS, GEMS, AND RELICS
Three giant rooms lined with jewelry cabinets make up the Third Courtyard's **Imperial Treasury.** A section is housed between the sultan's former hamam (peek skyward in the first room on the right to see the stained-glass ceiling). As you shuffle between the display cases watch for ruby-studded aigrettes that the sultans wore on their turbans. Then jostle with the crowds for a glimpse of the most expensive exhibit: the **Spoonmaker's Diamond.** At 86 carats, it's the world's fourth largest cut diamond. Seek out the **Topkapı Dagger** before you leave.

Directly opposite the Imperial Treasury is the **Chamber of the Sacred Relics.** The first room to the left contains part of the Prophet Mohammed's beard and one of his teeth. This is a place of pilgrimage for many pious visitors, so behave respectfully. Follow the interior trail onward past the ancient keys to the Ka'aba shrine in Mecca and one of Mohammed's finely inscribed swords.

■ FOURTH COURTYARD

Turn left out of the treasury and pad down the steps into the ungated **Fourth Courtyard.** The intricate kiosks and guardhouses let you know that you're standing in the most private section of the royal palace. Circle the high palace walls to get your bearings. Take in the sea views across to Asia that the sultans once enjoyed. Visit each of the ornate kiosks in turn. The **Baghdad Pavilion,** with its low sofas, open fireplace, and domed bloodred ceiling was a favorite spot for the sultans to relax. Peer inside the **Circumcision Room** to see some of the palace's most intricate İznik tiles.

Bab-ı Hümayun Caddesi · tel 0212 512 0480 · Closed Tues. · $$$ (harem, an additional $$) · Tram: Gülhane · topkapisarayi.gov.tr

Admiring the view from the marble terrace outside the Baghdad Pavilion

Ottoman Istanbul

Around the end of the 13th century, Osman, the leader of a group of nomadic Muslim Turks in Anatolia, established the state that would become the Ottoman Empire, with Istanbul as its capital. For almost half a millennium, ruling over vast domains in Europe, Africa, and Asia, the Ottoman sultans enriched the city with the magnificent mosques and palaces that remain among its most spectacular sights today.

A portrait of Sultan Mehmet II by Gentile Bellini
Opposite: The Court of Sultan Selim III at Topkapı Palace

Taking Constantinople

Aggressive warriors, the Ottomans crossed from Asia into Europe in the 14th century, conquering the Balkans. Only Christian Constantinople defied them, protected by its impregnable **City Walls** (see pp. 96–97). In 1451, young Sultan Mehmet II built the **Rumeli Fortress** (see p. 156) to dominate the Bosporus and prevent supplies or reinforcements reaching the Christians from the Black Sea. After a two-month siege, on May 29, 1453, the Turks took Constantinople.

Rebuilding the City

Mehmet found himself in possession of a city that was largely depopulated and in ruins. He set about transforming it into a suitable capital for his empire. Not only Turks but also Greeks, Armenians, and Jews were encouraged to move into the city. Mehmet established the **Grand Bazaar** (Kapalı Çarşı; see pp. 80–83) as a focus for reviving trade and encouraged Italian merchants to settle in

Galata (see pp. 110–114). Using the wealth generated by conquest and commerce, Mehmet built the **Topkapı Palace** (Topkapı Sarayı; see pp. 62–65)—imperial residence and seat of government.

Istanbul's Mosques

The Ottoman Empire reached its apogee in the 16th century, under Sultan Selim I (ruled 1512–1520) and his successor Süleyman the Magnificent (ruled 1520–1556). Ottoman armies conquered Egypt and Iraq and advanced into Europe. The Ottoman sultans were recognized as caliphs, the leaders of the Islamic world. With military conquest came cultural splendors. The Ottomans had initially created mosques by adapting Christian churches, as in the case of **Hagia Sophia** (Ayasofya Müzesi; see pp. 60–61). But, from Süleyman's time, they built the new mosques that dominate the Old City skyline today—most strikingly the vast **Süleymaniye Mosque**

(Süleymaniye Camii; see p. 76); the **Atik Valide Mosque** (Atik Valide Camii; see pp. 168–169); and the **Blue Mosque** (Sultan Ahmet Camii; see pp. 54–55).

Brutal Patrons

The Ottomans exhibited an extraordinary mix of refinement and brutality. For their mosques and the extensive development of the Topkapı Palace, they employed a wide range of artists and artisans, including calligraphers, carpet-weavers, silversmiths, and ceramicists creating richly colored glazed tiles. They beautified Istanbul with flower gardens, making a cult of tulips—Murad III had 300,000 tulip bulbs imported to the city in 1577. Yet cruelty and slavery were built into their

MIMAR **SINAN**

Mimar Sinan (ca 1490–1588) was a military engineer before becoming Sultan Süleyman I's chief architect at the age of 50. His first masterpiece was the **Şehzade Mosque** (Şehzade Camii), built as a memorial to Süleyman's son Şehzade Mehmet, in 1543. His style combined geometrical perfection of form with elegant decoration. His buildings range from the vast **Süleymaniye Mosque** complex to the small but perfect **Rüstem Paşa Mosque** (Rüstem Paşa Camii; see p. 79).

The inner courtyard of Mimar Sinan's Süleymaniye Mosque

system of government. For fear of disputes over the succession, all of a sultan's brothers were executed when he came to the throne. The mothers of the sultan's children were slave women guarded in the harem by slave eunuchs. The elite soldiers of the Ottoman army, the Janissaries, were Christian-born men who, as children, had been forcibly taken from their families to be raised as Muslims.

Toward Decline

By the late 17th century, sultans had ceased to lead their armies, instead rarely leaving the confines of the Topkapı Palace. Corruption was rife, and vicious intrigues in the harem determined who held effective power. The Janissaries were no longer elite soldiers but, rather, a conservative privileged body resistant to innovation. The Ottomans confronted the need for reform. In 1826, the Janissary corps was suppressed with great bloodshed, so that the army could be modernized. Under Abdülmecid I, from 1839, moves were made to reform the administration, the law, and the economy on Western lines. The **Dolmabahçe Palace** (Dolmabahçe Sarayı; see pp. 152–153) was built as a modern replacement for antiquated Topkapı. But it was all too little and too late. Defeat in World War I destroyed the Ottoman Empire. The last sultan, Mehmed VI, fled into exile in 1922.

An elegant Swan Fountain stands at the center of the Imperial Garden at the Dolmabahçe Palace.

Ancient Sites

Istanbul was conquered by Christian Crusaders in 1204 and Muslim Ottomans in 1453. Despite these incursions, much of the city's ancient heritage has remained remarkably intact. A number of Roman columns, Greek churches, and Byzantine relics still look as they did centuries—if not millennia—ago.

■ HAGIA EIRENE MUSEUM

This fourth-century church in the grounds of **Topkapı Palace** (Topkapı Sarayı; see pp. 62–65) in the Old City ranks as the oldest in Istanbul, and is one of few to have avoided conversion into a mosque. It has only recently reopened after a long spell off-limits. Once inside, gaze up at the giant cruciform cross above the narthex lobby. Owing to the excellent acoustics at Hagia Eirene (Aya İrini), concerts for Istanbul's annual **Istanbul Music Festival** (*June*) are held here.

Topkapı Sarayı • tel 0212 512 0480 • Closed Tues. • $$ • Tram: Gülhane • topkapisarayi.gov.tr

■ THE HIPPODROME

When Emperor Constantine moved the Roman capital to Istanbul in A.D. 324, his first act was to extend the already huge hippodrome in the Old City. He built his palace next door and walked directly to the imperial box when addressing 100,000-strong crowds. You can still make out the markings of the 1,500-foot-long (460 m) racetrack on At Meydanı. Charioteers raced around spoils of war lined up at the center. These included the ancient Egyptian **Obelisk of Theodosius** (Dikilitaş; see p. 32). Surrounding the circuit was a giant stone stadium lined with bleachers (see **Museum of Turkish & Islamic Art,** p. 104).

Tram: Sultanahmet

■ SEA WALLS

In the eighth century, the Byzantines lined the Old City coastline with thick walls, in order to protect themselves from ocean-borne enemies. You can see the remains of this structure when you visit the **Southern Golden Horn** (see pp. 96–97) or when peering down

THE OLD CITY

The southern face of the carved pedestal beneath the Obelisk of Theodosius in the Hippodrome

from **Topkapı Palace** (Topkapı Sarayı; see pp. 62–65). Although crumbling, dozens of the watchtowers that lined the waterfront are still visible. These sea defenses were effective until Mehmet the Conqueror arrived in 1453 (see pp. 66–69). His cannon shot away the Sea Walls protecting the Balat suburb and the Ottoman army moved in en masse.

Kennedy Caddesi, Seraglio Point

■ GREAT PALACE MOSAIC MUSEUM
The Byzantine emperors' Great Palace once stood on the site of the **Blue**
Mosque (Sultan Ahmet Camii; see pp. 54–55), just south of the ancient **Hippodrome**. By the time of Emperor Justinian, its courtyard floors were covered in vast mosaics. These intricate sixth-century designs were unearthed just decades ago and are now the focus of the Great Palace Mosaic Museum (Büyük Saray Mozaikleri Müzesi). Admire the giant stone patchwork of lions, tigers, and hunting and pastoral scenes from a raised viewing balcony, then head down a set of stone steps for a closer view.

Torun Sokak • tel 0212 518 1205 • Closed Mon. • $ • Tram: Sultanahmet

Grand Bazaar to Eminönü

This neighborhood is the heart of Istanbul's shopping district, with the busy halls of the Grand Bazaar to the south and the aroma-infused stalls of the Spice Market to the north. In the network of streets that tumble downhill between the two, are numerous vendors housed in ancient courtyards (hans). Thousands of local shoppers come here daily to barter for everything from children's T-shirts to wedding dresses to skeins of Turkish wool. Also here is one of Ottoman architect Sinan's masterpieces—the 16th-century Süleymaniye Mosque—and the Sirkeci Train Station, former terminus of the luxurious Orient Express. Add to this mix the Eminönü shoreline, a utopia for street snackers, and you have a vibrant, mercantile neighborhood.

◐ **Istanbul's atmospheric
Grand Bazaar, in which
you can buy everything
from fine-woven textiles
to gold jewelry and
Turkish ceramics.**

Grand Bazaar to Eminönü

Meander labyrinthine streets that are a paradise for shoppers, devotees of architecture, and history buffs alike.

❶ Süleymaniye Mosque (see pp. 76) Admire the breathtaking interior of Istanbul's second largest mosque. Exit the grounds to the south. Continue south on Fuat Paşa Caddesi and then Çadırcılar Caddesi.

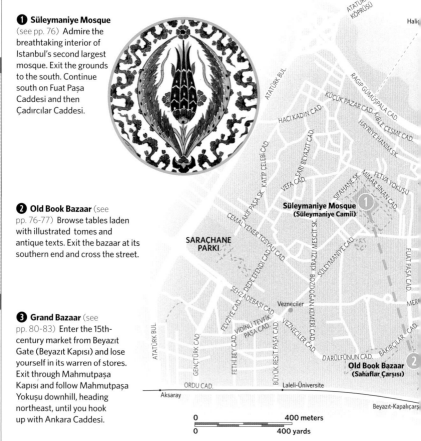

❷ Old Book Bazaar (see pp. 76-77) Browse tables laden with illustrated tomes and antique texts. Exit the bazaar at its southern end and cross the street.

❸ Grand Bazaar (see pp. 80-83) Enter the 15th-century market from Beyazıt Gate (Beyazıt Kapısı) and lose yourself in its warren of stores. Exit through Mahmutpaşa Kapısı and follow Mahmutpaşa Yokuşu downhill, heading northeast, until you hook up with Ankara Caddesi.

0 — 400 meters
0 — 400 yards

**GRAND BAZAAR TO EMINÖNÜ   DISTANCE: 2.5 MILES (4 KM)
TIME: APPROX. 7 HOURS   METRO START: VEZNECILER**

7 Tahtakale (see p. 79)
Pick up traditional Turkish homewares as gifts or souvenirs in this mecca for Turkish housewives.

6 Rüstem Paşa Mosque (see p. 79) Don't miss the mosque's arched entryway—off the main road and up a set of stairs. Take a close look at the floor-to-ceiling İznik tiles. Exit back onto Hasırcılar Caddesi, running through the north of Tahtakale.

5 Spice Market (see p. 78) Buy some edible treats to take home. Exit from the Spice Market's southwest corner, and walk northwest on Hasırcılar Caddesi.

4 Sirkeci Train Station (see p. 77) Peruse the 300 or so exhibits at the station's little museum. Head west on Hamidiye Caddesi to enter the Spice Market on Yeni Cami Caddesi.

GRAND BAZAAR TO EMINÖNÜ

Haliç

EMİNÖNÜ PORT

(Golden Horn)

GALATA KÖPRÜSÜ

Rüstem Paşa Mosque
(Rüstem Paşa Camii)

6

Eminönü

REŞADİYE CAD.

KENNEDY CAD.

Spice Market
(Mısır Çarşısı)

5

TAHTAKALE CAD.

BÜYÜK POSTANE CAD.

Sirkeci

Sirkeci Train Station
(Sirkeci Tren Garı)

4

SİRKECİ

AŞIR EFENDİ CAD.

7 Tahtakale

TAHTAKALE

CEMAL NADİR SK.

ANKARA CAD.

ÇAKMAKÇILAR YOKUŞU

MAHMUTPAŞA YOKUŞU

TARAKÇILAR CAD.

TÜRK OCAĞI CAD.

TİCARLAR SK.

ŞEREF EFENDİ SK.

BAB-I ALİ CAD.

3 Grand Bazaar
(Kapalı Çarşı)

YENİÇERİLER CAD.

Çemberlitaş

DİVAN YOLU CAD.

Süleymaniye Mosque

① Constructed between 1550 and 1557 under Sultan Süleyman the Magnificent, the Süleymaniye Mosque (Süleymaniye Camii) dominates the 17-acre (7 ha) complex that once included a medical school, *madrassa* religious school, hamam, library, and soup kitchen. On entering the gardens, look for the ten balconies that ring the mosque's four minarets in celebration of Süleyman as the Ottoman Empire's tenth sultan. Follow signs to the visitors' entrance through the mosque's vast courtyard. This wholly symmetrical building is the handiwork of the Ottoman Empire's chief architect, Mimar Sinan (see p. 68). Structural columns come from Baalbek in Lebanon and the city's own **Topkapı Palace** (Topkapı Sarayı; see pp. 62–65). Recent, extensive, renovations of the entire mosque have refreshed the building's 158-foot (48 m) dome, ornamental paintings, and colorful stained-glass windows. In the small cemetery at back, you'll find the octagonal, decoratively tiled mausoleums of Sultan Süleyman and his wife Roxelana. The architect Sinan is buried here, too, in a tiny tomb of his own just north of the complex at Mimar Sinan Caddesi and Fetva Yokuşu.

Mimar Sinan Caddesi • Closed Fri. a.m. and during prayer times (tombs closed Mon.) • Metro: Vezneciler; Tram: Beyazıt • suleymaniyecamii.org

Locals wash their hands and feet in preparation for entering the mosque to pray.

Old Book Bazaar

② The small, ancient Old Book Bazaar (Sahaflar Çarşısı) is piled high with Turkish volumes and texts catering to university students. Of primary interest to foreign visitors is the array of photo-heavy coffee-table books, and a selection of stunning framed and unframed Turkish miniatures. Originally pages in antique books, these miniatures are fine examples of Ottoman imagery. Although some authentic pieces fetch a fortune overseas, many dealers sell modern-day copies and prices should reflect this.

Çadırcılar Caddesi • Closed Sun. • Tram: Beyazıt

Grand Bazaar

3 See pp. 80–83.

Various entrances, including the main gates of Beyazıt Kapısı (Çadırcılar Caddesi) and Çarşı Kapısı (just north of Beyazıt Meydanı) • Closed Sun. • Tram: Beyazıt • grandbazaaristanbul.org

Sirkeci Train Station

4 Inaugurated in 1890, Sirkeci Train Station (Sirkeci Tren Garı) has long been known as the eastern terminus for history's most glamorous cross-European train line, the Orient Express. Today Sirkeci is a terminus of a different kind: Since 2013, it has been the place to jump aboard the subterranean Marmaray Metro line that dips beneath the Bosporus to Asia. The station itself is petite. Stroll along its ornate, East-meets-West facade, then pop indoors for a peek at the one-room **Istanbul Railway Museum** (İstanbul Demiryolu Müzesi; *tel 0212 520 7885, closed Mon. and Sun.*). This small space houses historical photographs and train memorabilia that includes dining services from the old Paris to Istanbul line. Next door to the museum, bow-tied waiters and traditional decor at the **Orient Express Restaurant** (*Sirkeci Gar İçi No. 2, tel 0212 522 2280*) evoke times past. The restaurant has remained popular since it opened in 1890.

Ankara Caddesi • tel 0212 527 1201 • Tram: Sirkeci

GOOD **EATS**

■ **DARÜZZIYAFE**
Traditional Turkish eats are dished up within the former kitchens of the Süleymaniye Mosque. Try simple spinach and cheese-filled *börek* or pastry-wrapped meatballs. **Şifahane Sokak 6, tel 0212 511 8414, $–$$**

■ **HAMDI**
Overlooking the Golden Horn, this high-end kebab specialist spills over three panoramic floors and serves grilled meat dishes from across the country. **Tahmis Caddesi, Kalçın Sokak 11, tel 0212 528 0390, $$**

■ **PANDELI RESTAURANT**
This elegant eatery sits directly above the Spice Market. *Hünkar beğendi* (roasted lamb on eggplant purée) is a house favorite. **Mısır Çarşısı 1, tel 0212 527 3909, $$**

Spice Market

5 Istanbul's Spice Market (Mısır Çarşısı, meaning Egyptian Bazaar) houses around 100 stores within its L-shaped arcade. Originally they may have sold herbs and spices exclusively, but today, many of these vendors also purvey dried fruits and superb Turkish delight *(lokum)*. Favorites include spicy red pepper flakes *(kırmızı pul biber)*, dried mint, and a wide variety of dried vegetables, from okra to eggplant. Big spenders can pick up niche items like Iranian saffron and top-quality caviar. The vibe here is easygoing, and most vendors are very happy to let you try before you buy. Many of them also have machines for vacuum-packing everything from loose tea to sumac. Don't limit yourself to shopping solely within the Spice Market. Its external western wall is lined with vendors selling cheeses, olives, and dried meats from across Anatolia (see also p. 25).

Entrances on Ragıp Gümüşpala Caddesi, Tahmis Sokak, Çiçek Pazarı Sokak, and Yeni Cami Caddesi • Tram: Eminönü

Whether walnut- or pistachio-filled, flaky, fresh *baklava* is a must-buy at the Spice Market.

Rüstem Paşa Mosque

6 Perhaps the most enchanting of Istanbul's mosques, Rüstem Paşa Mosque (Rüstem Paşa Camii) was designed by royal architect Mimar Sinan (see p. 68) and constructed in 1561. It was dedicated to Sultan Süleyman the Magnificent's grand vizier (prime minister), Rüstem Paşa, who was also his close friend and son-in-law. Ascend one of the mosque's two winding staircases to an arcaded outdoor terrace area. It's here that you'll have an immediate inkling as to what makes this place of worship so special. The mosque is covered—both inside and out—in beautiful, hand-painted, blue İznik tiles. Take advantage of this opportunity to examine the tiles in detail—this is one of few places in Istanbul where visitors are allowed such close proximity. Keep an eye out for those decorated in deep red tones, too: This particular pigment was added only by the city's most skilled artisans.

Hasırcılar Caddesi • Closed during prayer times • Tram: Eminönü

IN **THE KNOW**

İznik tiles are a feature of the grandest Istanbul mosques, and were handmade by the famed artisans of İznik, a town 90 miles (145 km) to the east. The ceramic design was first influenced by Chinese patterns, but by the 16th century, the Turks had added their own symmetry in bold shades of red, turquoise, and cobalt blue. Popular patterns of the day include tulips, blossoms, and leaping fish.

Tahtakale

7 Stepping out of **Rüstem Paşa Mosque,** you'll find yourself in the bustling district of Tahtakale—a labyrinth of busy, narrow, pedestrianized streets filled with shops selling all manner of household goods. This area is a favorite with serious Turkish shoppers and is particularly well known for its wealth of woodenwares—from chopping boards and oversized stirring spoons to ornate, handcrafted backgammon (*tavla*) sets. The area is also a great place to pick up sets of traditional tulip-shaped tea glasses, Turkish coffee pots, and double-stacked Turkish teapots.

Streets surrounding Hasırcılar Caddesi and Uzunçarşı Caddesi • Tram: Eminönü

Grand Bazaar

Take your pick of 4,000 stores selling everything from leather goods, lighting, and jewelry to İznik tiles and fine Turkish textiles.

Colored glass lamps and lanterns sparkle like gems at the Grand Bazaar.

Many historians claim that Istanbul's Grand Bazaar (Kapalı Çarşı) is the world's first shopping mall. Construction of the original trading halls (*bedestens*) started in 1461 under Sultan Mehmet the Conqueror. This covered marketplace expanded over the years. The caravansaries (inns with courtyards) and narrow alleyways between the halls were soon swallowed up. Süleyman the Magnificent added extensions a century later. The main entrance sits just off Divan Yolu Caddesi, the ancient road from Constantinople to Rome.

THE OLD AND THE NEW

On entering the Grand Bazaar, look up, and you'll see that many of its ceilings are painted with traditional motifs in red and blue. But there's a nod to the 21st century too, with suspended flat-screen TVs advertising various shops. As you explore the place, you'll come across the market's four bubbling fountains, where vendors and locals often stop to splash their hands and faces in summer.

FINDING YOUR WAY

Everywhere you look, the Grand Bazaar is littered with signage, from panels indicating specific streets to areas and sections. Although helpful, it is easier to pick up a streetmap from one of the marketplace's stores. (Note that not all vendors stock these maps.)

Whether you're in the market for ceramics from Kütahya and İznik (Turkey's twin pottery capitals), butter-soft leather handbags, brightly colored glass lanterns, luxuriant pashmina scarves, or Middle Eastern antiques, the Grand Bazaar truly has it all. Simply wander the atmospheric alleyways and see what strikes your fancy. You'll soon notice that within the market, vendors are generally grouped together into districts according to their wares.

FROM JEWELRY TO COPPERWARE

Start on **Kalpakçilarbaşi Caddesi,** famed for its jewelry stores, among them **Boybeyi Jewelry** *(nos. 151 and 163, tel 0212 522 4446).* This family-run business has been producing rose-cut diamonds and designs inspired by Turkish culture for 100 years.

Turning left on to **Kolancılar Sokak** will take you northward to **İç Bedesten** (also known as Cevahir Bedesteni), the Grand Bazaar's original vaulted trading hall and the heart of the market. The trading hall is constructed above the city's Roman agora, and legend has it that subterranean tunnels connect this structure to the nearby **Spice Market** (Mısır Çarşısı; see p. 78). Today İç Bedesten's high-end kiosks purvey antiques, copperware, icons, and exquisite vintage watches.

Row upon row of Turkish gold bracelets glimmer in the market's jewelry district.

■ CERAMICS & TEXTILES

Exit İç Bedesten to the north onto **Sahaflar Bedesteni Sokak.** West of here sits the market's general souvenirs section. If ceramics are your passion, veer left for a stop at **EM-ER Seramik & Çini** (*Takkeciler Sokak 100, tel 0212 514 2265*). Wares range from tiny tiles adorned with tulips to elegant serving platters. All are designed and hand-painted in Kütahya.

Stroll westward and you'll soon hit **Yağlıkçılar Caddesi.** This north-south street is lined with stores selling textiles of all types, from delicate batik scarves and mohair wraps to bathroom linens. For classic woven hamam towels, head to **Azad Tekstil** (*Yağlıkçılar Caddesi 16, tel 0212 512 4202*). On the same street, **Semerkand** (*Yağlıkçılar Caddesi, Astarcı Han 25–32, tel 0212 526 2269*) is packed with one-of-a-kind regional textiles, including colorful Ottoman kaftans. Nearby **İgüs** (*Yağlıkçılar Caddesi 80, tel 0212 512 3528*) sells a stunning selection of silky pashminas and wool wraps.

Make your way to the opposite side of the market, following **Halıcılar**

Caddesi eastward. **Adnan & Hasan** (*Halıcılar Caddesi 89–92, tel 0212 527 9887*) is one of the Grand Bazaar's longest established shops, specializing in a wide range of Anatolian carpets and kilims. For olive-oil soaps infused with rose and jasmine oils, pop into nearby **Abdulla Natural Ürünler** (*Halıcılar Caddesi 58–60, tel 0212 527 3684*) on the way.

Turn left onto **Kuyumcular Caddesi.** Follow the street all the way north to find **Zincirli Han,** one of the bazaar's prettiest hans, or ancient inns used for trading. Today the courtyard is painted an attractive pink, and is home to carpet and kilim vendor **Şişko Osman** (*Zincirli Han 15, tel 0212 528 3548*).

■ Weekly Auctions

Backtrack onto Kuyumcular Caddesi, following it southward. Just east of here sits the domed **Sandal Bedesten,** the Grand Bazaar's second oldest section, which hosts public carpet auctions on Wednesdays (*1 p.m.*). Alternatively, you can continue strolling due south. Straight ahead, fur and leatherwear vendors cluster in the bazaar's **Kürkçüler Çarsısı.**

■ Market Refreshments

Need to take the load off your toes? Take **Yağlıkçılar Caddesi** south to **Sarı Hacı Hasan Sokak.** Make a right, then your first left to find **Havuzlu** (*Gani Çelebi Sokak 3, tel 0212 527 3346*), the bazaar's 50-year-old restaurant, which serves up traditional Turkish fare. Alternatively, for a lighter bite, stop by the **Fes Cafe** (*Halıcılar Caddesi 58–62, tel 0212 528 1613*) for a cup of Turkish coffee and a snack.

Various entrances, including the main gates of Beyazıt Kapısı (Çadırcılar Caddesi) and Çarşı Kapısı (just north of Beyazıt Meydanı) • Closed Sun. • Tram: Beyazıt • grandbazaaristanbul.org

GRAND BAZAAR TO EMINÖNÜ

City of Merchants

Istanbul's unique geographical position, straddling both the Asian and the European banks of the Bosporus, gave the city unrivaled strategic power for many centuries. Those ruling the city also had control over the waterway—at one time a major conduit on the Silk Road. For more than a millennium, therefore, Istanbul played a significant role in the movement of ideas, traditions, crafts, and, above all, goods from East to West.

The construction of Haydarpaşa Station on the Asian shores of the Bosporus in 1872 meant that goods could be loaded directly onto boats from trains and vice versa.
Opposite: One of several trading hans flanking Istanbul's Grand Bazaar

Ancient Traders

By A.D. 500, Constantinople (as Istanbul was then known) was the largest city the world had ever seen. The Bosporus connected the Black Sea in the north to the Mediterranean in the south, making the city a natural hub on the trade routes that carried all manner of goods from China in Asia to Rome in Europe, and vice versa. Navigating the waterway's currents for at least 1,350 years, many thousands of merchants passed through Istanbul with their precious cargoes.

Ottoman Trends

Goods traveled overland, too, and in the streets surrounding the warren-like trading halls of the **Grand Bazaar** (Kapalı Çarşı; see pp. 80–83) established by Sultan Mehmet I in 1461, numerous caravansaries (inns with courtyards) offered passing merchants cool and quiet pit stops for rest and refreshment. These locales also offered an opportunity to trade. Over time, these courtyards became trading hans in their own right and many continue to function as such.

Walk the streets of Istanbul today, and you'll find entire districts dedicated to specific goods, just as they have been in the Grand Bazaar for centuries, from the tight-knit streets of domestic wares in **Tahtakale** (see p. 79) to the hardware stores of **Perşembe Pazarı** (see p. 37). East of Sultanahmet lies the fabric district, while the shops on the southwestern slopes below **Galata Tower** (Galata Kulesi; see pp. 110–111) sell only lighting. Such districts are not unheard of in other major cities—consider New York's garment or meatpacking districts—yet many exist in name alone, having succumbed to trendy retail developers. This is not so in Istanbul, and for the time being at least, trade remains very much a part of the city's identity.

THE **SILK ROAD**

Operating primarily during the Byzantine era (ca 130 B.C. to A.D. 1453), and taking its name from China's most coveted export at the time, the Silk Road was not just one, but several routes that facilitated the widespread transportation of goods across much of Asia Minor and Europe. Among the items traded were woven silk; porcelain and lacquerware from China; Egyptian glassware; and saffron from Persia (now Iran).

Street Food

Istanbullus are passionate foodies who always have time for a snack, whether it's a *simit* bread roll at breakfast or stuffed mussels gulped on the go. While the Eminönü shoreline, near the Spice Market, is one of Istanbul's top street-food destinations, popular street eats are scattered throughout the city.

■ FISH SANDWICH

The *balık ekmek* fish sandwich is sold all along the banks of the Bosporus and the Golden Horn. However it is the southern end of the **Galata Bridge** (Galata Köprüsü; see pp. 113–114) on the Eminönü shoreline that functions as a nexus for this popular lunch. Wooden Ottoman-style boats are moored to the shoreline with chefs turning out sandwiches—a mix of grilled mackerel, chopped onion, and lettuce, served on crusty white bread—at lightning speed. Don't even think about ordering off menu! Grab your order, then find a spot at one of the tiny tables. For a local twist, head to the nearby kiosk for some pickled vegetables (*turşu*) on the side.

■ STUFFED MUSSELS

Popular since Ottoman times, stuffed mussels (*midye dolma*) are packed with a mix of pine nuts, raisins, warming spices, and rice. They're laid out on large platters, and served with a big squeeze of lemon. Order them one at a time and eat your fill. Keep an eye out for busy stands with a high turnover—these are your best bet for ensuring the freshest of mussels. You'll see popular vendors lined up on the waterfront in the Karaköy neighborhood.

■ TATLI

Turks have a sweet tooth, so it's little surprise that desserts (*tatlı*) prove just as popular on the go. Street vendors specializing in sweet treats are often loaded up with sticky semolina (*tulumba*) and pistachio-topped *şambali* sponge cake, as well as other syrup-soaked delights. Particularly crowd-pleasing carts cluster in the Galata neighborhood—at the northern end of the **Galata Bridge** and just beneath the **Galata Tower** (Galata Kulesi; see pp. 110–111).

Simit rolls and roasted chestnuts are sold from red mobile kiosks across the whole city.

■ İÇLİ KÖFTE

İçli köfte consist of a crunchy bulgur wheat shell stuffed with ground lamb, onions, and spices. These savory snacks are perfect afternoon fuel. See if you can spot the celebrated street vendor on **İstiklal Caddesi** (see pp. 134–135) in the Beyoğlu neighborhood (diagonally opposite Galatasaray High School).

■ ROASTED NIBBLES

Regardless of the season—or time of day—roasted chestnuts and corn on the cob are also popular street foods.

Both are sold from government-sponsored mobile kiosks, and can be found throughout Beyoğlu, Sultanahmet, and along the shores of the Golden Horn.

■ SIMIT

A close cousin of the bagel and popular in Istanbul for more than five centuries, these sesame-topped loops of bread frequently function as breakfast on the run. From shop managers to bankers, Istanbul's commuters can all be seen grabbing one of these wallet-friendly treats en route to work.

SOUTHERN
GOLDEN HORN

Istanbul Boğazı (Bosporus)

*Marmara Denizi
(Sea of Marmara)*

Southern Golden Horn

The three historic suburbs of Fatih, Fener, and Eyüp are just a mile or two from the glitz of downtown Istanbul, but they could not be more different in character. Between them, these neighborhoods are home to more significant mosques, churches, and synagogues than almost any other city on Earth, and stand testimony to the religious tolerance of the Ottoman sultans. Not to be missed are some of the world's finest frescoes inside the Chora Church. A number of sights here—the City Walls and the Church of St. Mary of the Mongols, are crumbling, and some of the streets around the Yavuz Sultan Selim Mosque are poorly signposted. Yet each prayer hall or chapel shines with authenticity and, often as not, is gilded with gold.

◀ **Inside the Chora Church.
Almost every surface
bears a mosaic or fresco
of exceptional quality.**

Southern Golden Horn

Explore the intricacies of Istanbul's religious makeup through its mosques, churches, and synagogues.

❽ Eyüp (see p. 97) Ride the funicular up to the Pierre Loti cable-car station and explore the neighborhood.

❹ Greek Orthodox Patriarchal Church of St. George (see pp. 94–95) Study the screen of icons at this important Greek Orthodox church. Retrace your steps on Yıldırım Caddesi.

❺ Yavuz Sultan Selim Mosque (see p. 93) Examine the finer details of this richly decorated hilltop mosque. Retrace your steps on Sultan Selim Caddesi, fork steeply down the unsigned Camcı Çeşmesi Yokuşu to Yıldırım Caddesi, then turn right.

❼ City Walls (see pp. 96–97) The third-century land walls, come into sight as you approach. Follow the walls northeast until you reach the Golden Horn seafront. Hail a cab from Ayvansaray Caddesi to Eyüp's cable-car station.

HALİÇ PARKİ

İSTANBUL ÇEVRE YOLU

ŞABAN DERESİ SK.

KUMBARAHANE CAD

KARAAĞAÇ CAD.

SİLAHTARAĞA CAD.

HALİÇ KÖPRÜSÜ

Haliç

YAVEDUT CAD.

SİLAHTARAĞA CAD.

❽ Eyüp

BÜLBÜLDERE CAD

EYÜP MEZARLIĞI (CEMETERY)

FAHRİ KORUTÜRK CAD.

EYÜP

EYÜP SULTAN BUL.

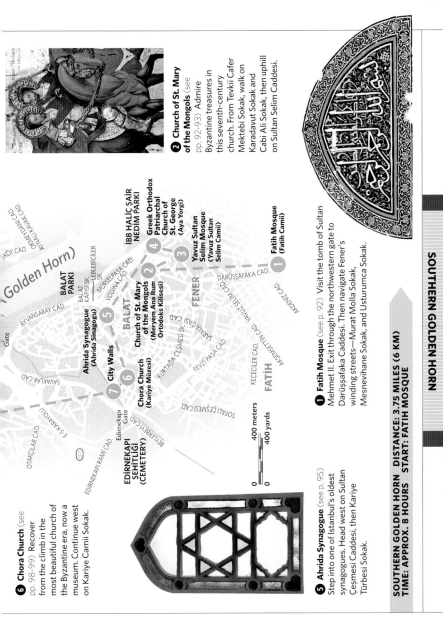

6 Chora Church (see pp. 98-99) Recover from the climb in the most beautiful church of the Byzantine era, now a museum. Continue west on Kariye Camii Sokak.

2 Church of St. Mary of the Mongols (see pp. 92-93) Admire Byzantine treasures in this seventh-century church. From Tevkii Cafer Mektebi Sokak, walk on Karadavut Sokak and Cabi Ali Sokak, then uphill on Sultan Selim Caddesi.

ANITKAVRAM CAD.
KÖY. CAD.
ANITKAVRAM CAD.
(Golden Horn)
SAVAKLAR CAD.
AYVANSARAY CAD.
Gate
OTAKCILAR CAD.
E-5 KARAYOLU
EDIRNEKAPI RAMI CAD.
Edirnekapı Gate
BEYLERBEYI CAD.
0260

Ahrida Synagogue (Ahrida Sinagogu)
5 City Walls
7 City Walls
Chora Church (Kariye Müzesi)
6 Chora Church

BALAT PARKI
BALAT KAPISI SK.
LEBLEBICILER SK.
MÜRSELPAŞA CAD.
VODINA CAD.

Church of St. Mary of the Mongols (Meryem Ana Rum Ortodoks Kilisesi)
2

BALAT
KURTAĞA ÇEŞMESI SK.
SARAÇAĞASI CAD.

IBB HALIÇ ŞAIR NEDIM PARKI
Greek Orthodox Church of St. George (Aya Yorgi)
4

FENER
DARÜŞŞAFAKA CAD.

Yavuz Sultan Selim Mosque (Yavuz Sultan Selim Camii)
3

YAVUZ SELIM CAD.
AKDENIZ CAD.

Fatih Mosque (Fatih Camii)
1

FEVZI PAŞA CAD.
KEÇECILER CAD.
AKŞEMSETTIN CAD.

FATİH

SOFALI ÇEŞME SOKAK

EDIRNEKAPI ŞEHITLIĞI (CEMETERY)

EDIRNEKAPI RAMI CAD.
Edirnekapı Gate
BEYLERBEYI CAD.

0 ——— 400 meters
0 ——— 400 yards

6 Chora Church (see pp. 98-99) Recover from the climb in the most beautiful church of the Byzantine era, now a museum. Continue west on Kariye Camii Sokak.

5 Ahrida Synagogue (see p. 95) Step into one of Istanbul's oldest synagogues. Head west on Sultan Çeşmesi Caddesi, then Kariye Türbesi Sokak.

1 Fatih Mosque (see p. 92) Visit the tomb of Sultan Mehmet II. Exit through the northwestern gate to Darüşşafaka Caddesi. Then navigate Fener's winding streets—Murat Molla Sokak, Mesnevihane Sokak, and Usturumca Sokak.

SOUTHERN GOLDEN HORN

SOUTHERN GOLDEN HORN DISTANCE: 3.75 MILES (6 KM)
TIME: APPROX. 8 HOURS START: FATIH MOSQUE

SOUTHERN GOLDEN HORN

SAVVY **TRAVELER**

If visiting Fatih on a Wednesday, make a detour to the bustling **Çarşamba Pazarı** *(Fatih Caddesi, 5 a.m.–9 p.m.)* street market that sprawls through the network of streets to the north of Fatih Mosque. With more than 1,000 vendors this is one of Istanbul's biggest markets, yet is rarely visited by tourists. It's a rough-and-tumble affair in which you'll find everything from clothing to eggs and from hardware to seasonal fruit.

Fatih Mosque

1 Built on Istanbul's highest hill, Fatih Mosque (Fatih Camii) is dedicated to the Ottoman hero Mehmet the Conqueror (see pp. 66–69), who ordered its construction in the mid-15th century—on the site of the Church of the Holy Apostles, founded by Constantine the Great. Walk around the four walls of the mosque complex, and you'll soon understand the building's importance. As Istanbul's first imperial mosque, the dimensions are meant to shock and awe. Wander through the impressive arch leading into the mosque's inner courtyard. Much of the complex was destroyed by an earthquake in 1766, but the courtyard survived. At its center, you'll see the original fountain *(şadırvan),* with its gilt decoration and conical roof.

Much of the mosque itself was damaged by the earthquake, and what you see today is a 1771 remodeling. The 85-foot-high (26 m) dome is supported by four semidomes, all held up by columns of solid marble. Before leaving the complex, seek out Mehmet's tomb, which lies beside the mosque's southeastern walls. Pilgrims come from miles around to pay their respects.

Darüşşafaka Caddesi • Closed during prayer times • Bus: 35D, 36A, 90

Church of St. Mary of the Mongols

2 Few visitors venture this far into the ancient Greek enclave of Fener to see this enchanting relic. The seventh-century Church of St. Mary of the Mongols (Meryem Ana Rum Ortodoks Kilisesi) is the only Byzantine church in Istanbul never to have been converted into a mosque. Although the church is generally closed to the public, if you ring the door bell, the attendant will let you in.

On entering, the church's hushed tones make you feel as if you're part of a history barely changed in 13 centuries. Notice the painting of the *Last Judgment* as you step inside the narthex (lobby). A few steps farther along is a place to light a beeswax candle (and perhaps pass a few coins to the attendant at the same time). Prepare yourself for the wealth of silver votives and golden icons that ring the altar, among them a mosaic portrait of the Virgin Mary, or *Theotokos* (in Greek).

Firketeci Sokak, Fener • $ (donation) • Bus: 35D

Yavuz Sultan Selim Mosque

3 The second oldest of Istanbul's imperial mosques, the Yavuz Sultan Selim Mosque (Yavuz Sultan Selim Camii) was dedicated to Süleyman the Magnificent's empire-expanding father, Sultan Selim I, and it shows. The mosque is ambitious in every possible way. Begin your visit in the open-air courtyard. Notice the half moons of intricate İznik tiles that grace every single portico. Each is a different style. Inside, the mosque's walls are lined with polished stone, not modern plasterwork, and mother-of-pearl marquetry embellishes the woodwork. The complex's crowning glory are its north-facing gardens. Hanging high above the Golden Horn, the gardens are home to two octagonal tombs. One—topped with a ridged dome—is that of Selim I; another houses four of Süleyman's children.

Sultan Selim Caddesi • Closed during prayer times • Bus: 35D, 36A, 90

The vast space beneath Yavuz Sultan Selim Mosque's shallow dome

Orthodox patriarchs assemble to discuss matters of faith at the Church of St. George.

Greek Orthodox Patriarchal Church of St. George

4 Behind three storys of fine stonework sits the Greek Orthodox Patriarchal Church of St. George (Aya Yorgi), seat of the senior patriarchate who presides over the world's 300 million adherents of the Greek Orthodox faith. From the shady courtyard, head inside to light a candle in the vestibule; the walnut, ivory-inlaid candle stand dates from the 17th century. Opposite are paintings of St. George (the faith's Great Martyr) slaying the dragon. Pass through the small door near the candles to reach the nave of the church, suffused with silence and smoke from incense. Chandeliers cast an eerie light over the scene. Scores of shimmering religious icons line the three interior walls. Some of them predate the fabulous frescoes inside the **Hagia Sophia** (Ayasofya Müzesi; see pp. 60–61) and the **Chora Church** (Kariye Müzesi; see pp. 98–99). To the right of the wall of icons lies a black fragment of the **Pillar of the Flagellation,** believed to be the original column to which Christ was tied before his crucifixion. At the far end of the church sits the patriarch's marble throne, standing 13 feet (4 m) tall and made from walnut inlaid with ivory and mother-of-pearl.

Dr. Sadık Ahmet Caddesi · tel 0212 521 1921 · Bus: 35D, 48E, 55T, 99A · patriarchate.org

Ahrida Synagogue

5 The stroll from the **Greek Orthodox Patriarchal Church of St. George** to the Ahrida Synagogue (Ahrida Sinagogu) leads through the heart of Fener, a charming network of narrow, cobbled streets whose wooden houses—many painted in bright colors—have seen better days. En route, the Vodina Caddesi opens on the right to reveal the ancient sea walls and the Golden Horn beyond. You may only visit the Ahrida Synagogue (*weekday mornings*) with prior emailed permission from Istanbul's Turkish Jewish Community. Inside, a boat-shaped prayer deck dominates the central space. Some say it honors Noah's ark, others that it reminds the congregation of the flight from Spain during the Inquisition.

Kürkçü Çeşmesi Sokak · Bus: 35D, 48E, 55T, 99A · turkyahudileri.com

Chora Church

6 (see pp. 98–99)
Kariye Camii Sokak 26 · tel 0212 518 1021 · Closed Wed. · $$ · Bus: 28, 36A, 39D, 88A · kariye.muze.gov.tr

The Ahrida Synagogue's holy ark in which the Torah scrolls are stored when not in use.

City Walls

7 Istanbul's city walls were built by Emperor Theodosius in
A.D. 413—just in time to keep Attila the Hun from rampaging
through Istanbul. The 96 defensive towers still stretch from the
Sea of Marmara to the Golden Horn. You're welcome to hike along
them or even climb one or two at your own risk (the views are
fabulous, but the crumbling stonework and lack of railings add an
element of peril). Bear in mind, also, that they run through one of
Istanbul's humblest neighborhoods.

Walk the southwest–northeast section from Edirnekapı Gate
to Ayvansaray Gate. On the hill behind you'll see the **Mihrimah
Sultan Mosque** (Mihrimah Sultan Camii), the second mosque

**A section of the Byzantine city
walls, close to Edirnekapı Gate**

named for Sultan Süleyman the Magnificent's favorite daughter (for the first, see p. 163). Walk downhill for ten minutes to arrive at the handsome facade of the former Byzantine **Palace of the Porphyrogenitus** (Tekfur Sarayı). Derelict since the late 17th century, the palace is now undergoing renovation.

Ten more minutes, and a short detour east on Eğrikapı Caddesi then north on Dervişzade Sokak leads to the **İvaz Efendi Mosque** (Kazasker İvaz Efendi Camii) with fabulous İznik tiles in its *mihrab*. A tiny dervish lodge, the **Emir Buhari Dervish Lodge** (Emir Buhari Tekkesi) is just down the street to your right. Your route ends at the more recent **Sea Walls** (see pp. 70–71), which weren't enough to keep Sultan Mehmet the Conqueror's battleships at bay in 1453.

Hoca Çakır Caddesi • Bus: 35D, 48E, 55T, 99A

Eyüp

Best reached via cable car (Piyerloti Teleferik; $), this district's highest point is where French author Pierre Loti (after whom both the hill and its funicular are named) sought inspiration, with the Golden Horn rippling in the distance. Walk downhill from the observation deck to the **Eyüp Sultan Mosque** (Eyüp Sultan Camii, *Eyüp Sultan Bulvarı*). The Eyüp for whom the district is named was one of Prophet Mohammed's friends who fell while holding the Islamic banner during the Arab siege of Istanbul 1,300 years ago. His tomb here is a place of pilgrimage. Notice, above the door, the golden Arabic script telling of Eyüp's deeds. On your way to the mosque, you'll pass through the hauntingly beautiful Muslim graveyard that descends to the Golden Horn. Enjoy the shade and the views.

İdris Köşkü Caddesi & Türbe Sokak • Funicular: Eyüp

GOOD **EATS**

■ **ASITANE**
A luxurious eatery by the Chora Church that serves classic Ottoman dishes under the watchful eye of "food archaeologist" Engin Türker. **Kariye Camii Sokak 63, tel 0212 635 7997, $$$**

■ **CAFÉ VODINA**
Come here for homemade pastries and jams, or lunchtime Turkish ravioli (*mantı*), all served up in a historic townhouse. **Vodina Caddesi 39, tel 0212 531 0057, $**

■ **DERVIŞ BABA**
This vintage coffee house —which naturally also sells gallons of tea—hosts traditional Turkish singers and makes a great pit stop between sights. **Kürkçü Çeşmesi Sokak 10, tel 0539 719 1959, $**

SOUTHERN GOLDEN HORN

Chora Church

The discovery of ancient frescoes and mosaics less than a century ago put this little-known church on the map.

The scenes depicted in the Chora Church frescoes are remarkably realistic for their time.

When the Chora Church (Kariye Müzesi) was turned into a mosque in around 1500, the conversion included plastering over a gallery of frescoes and mosaics that had been created in the early 1300s. This protective covering kept the works in good condition until they were revealed and first restored 70 years ago. Covering almost all visible surfaces, the artworks depict scenes from the life of Christ—his infancy, his ministry, and his ancestry—and include portraits of the Virgin Mary and the Saints Peter and Paul.

■ BIBLE STORIES

The main entrance to the church leads into the exonarthex (outer lobby). Here, you can follow a New Testament fresco tour from **Joseph's journey to Bethlehem** through the **Nativity Story** to **John the Baptist's witness of Christ.** Be sure to look above the main entrance for the half-ruined mosaic depicting the **Miracles of Christ,** in which the turning of water into wine and the feeding of the 5,000 are shown in intricate detail.

■ ST. PETER AND ST. PAUL

Proceed to the esonarthex (inner lobby), which runs parallel to the exonarthex but is smaller and more atmospheric. The lives of the apostles Peter (holding the keys to heaven) and Paul (giving the sign of the blessing) are displayed on opposite panels leading up to the naos (nave).

Turn around to see a depiction of Christ Pantocrator and the Virgin Mary, which features on the arch above the entrance. Look closely at the child Christ on the medallion worn by Mary. It is said to symbolize the bosom of Mary as larger than the universe. Farther into the esonarthex, episodes

from the life of the Virgin Mary are chronicled in three deep bays.

■ STEPS TO HEAVEN

On entering the naos, immediately turn around to see the **Dormition of the Virgin** (Assumption of Mary) above the entrance—a medley of gold and blue. In the fresco, the haloed Christ holds an infant (representing Mary's soul) as he pays his final respects to her. Look up to the golden dome to see the **Genealogy of Christ,** depicting 24 of his early ancestors.

■ DEATH AND RESURRECTION

Yet more frescoes, this time dealing with Christ's miraculous resurrection, are located in the Pareeclesion side chapel a few steps south.

Kariye Camii Sokak 26 · tel 0212 518 1021 · Closed Wed. · $$ · Bus: 28, 36A, 39D, 88A · kariye.muze.gov.tr

Byzantine Istanbul

For 1,000 years, the city now known as Istanbul was Constantinople, the largest city in the Christian world and capital of the illustrious Byzantine Empire. The city was was founded by, and named for, the Roman emperor, Constantine the Great, and it served as the capital of the Roman Empire in the East. Today, the spirit of this lost empire has survived in an awe-inspiring legacy of art and architecture.

Celebrating Sunday mass at the Greek Orthodox Patriarchal Church of St. George Opposite: Hagia Sophia's mosaic of the Virgin Mary holding the infant Jesus. She is flanked by the Emperors Constantine and Justinian.

Roman Roots

The Byzantine Empire was a continuation of the ancient Roman Empire. After the fall of the city of Rome to barbarian invaders in A.D. 476, the emperors in Constantinople still thought of themselves as Romans. But by the time of Emperor Justinian, who ruled from A.D. 527 to 565, the Eastern Roman Empire was already evolving into something strange and distinctive: Greek was its official language instead of Latin; its society and culture were dominated by the Christian Church; and it was influenced by Asiatic models of government, in which rulers sustained the mystique of power through elaborate rituals and lavish displays of wealth.

The Hagia Sophia

To form an idea of the scale and magnificence of the Byzantine Empire, you only need look at one of the city's most famous buildings, the basilica of **Hagia Sophia** (Ayasofya Müzesi; see pp. 60–61).

SOUTHERN GOLDEN HORN

Built under Justinian in A.D. 537 and embellished over the following centuries, it was by far the largest church in the world at that time, advertising Constantinople's claim to replace Rome as the center of Christianity. The rich materials used in its construction were brought from across Justinian's extensive empire—from Egypt and from Syria as well as from modern-day Turkey and Greece.

Palace Grandeur

Little now remains of the nearby palace complex from which the Byzantine emperors ruled, although some idea of its size can be gained from the impressive scale of the **Basilica Cistern** (Yerebatan Sarnarcı; see pp. 56–57) that provided its water supply. The mosaic pavement preserved in

KEY **DATES**

527-565 Reign of Emperor Justinian sees transition from Roman to Byzantine Empire

674-678 Arabs besiege Constantinople

726-842 Byzantine authorities try to ban icons

867 Basil I founds the Macedonian dynasty

1071 Byzantine army suffers severe defeat by Turks at the battle of Manzikert

1081 Alexios I founds the Comnenian dynasty

1204 Constantinople is sacked during Fourth Crusade

1453 Constantinople falls to the Ottoman Turks; end of the Byzantine Empire

SOUTHERN GOLDEN HORN

A mosaic from the Chora Church depicting St. Paul. He holds the gospel in his left hand while making the gesture of a blessing with his right.
Opposite: Italian artist Jacopo Robusti Tintoretto's "Capture of Constantinople" in 1204

the **Great Palace Mosaic Museum** (Büyük Saray Mozaikleri Müzesi; see p. 71) gives an idea of its style of decoration—more ancient Roman art than Byzantine.

In front of the palace was the **Hippodrome** (see p. 70), a focus of popular entertainment where horse and chariot races were held. These events excited passionate interest in the city's population and, in A.D. 532, were the occasion for the Nika riots, the worst civil disturbance in Byzantine history. Supporters of the rival Blue and Green chariot teams engaged in fighting that destroyed a large part of the city and caused the deaths of 30,000 people. The shape of the Hippodrome is still visible in the gardens of Sultanahmet Meydanı.

Flourishing Cultural City

The early centuries of the Byzantine Empire were a time of troubles. The Byzantines were beset by enemies, including the Persians, the Bulgars, and, most dangerously, the Arabs. Inspired by the new faith of Islam, Arab armies besieged Constantinople. Although they failed to penetrate the Theodosian Walls and were eventually repulsed, the Muslims held on to North Africa and the eastern Mediterranean, which were lost to the Byzantine Empire for good.

The internal affairs of the Empire were equally disturbed. Byzantine political life was notorious for its vicious intrigues and instability. Many emperors died violent deaths, some in foreign wars but more at the hands of rivals at home. Yet, against the odds, Constantinople flourished. One of the wealthiest cities in the world, from the ninth century onward it was enriched with a host of new or rebuilt churches, decorated by the finest artists in glittering mosaics. Many of these buildings have since been rendered almost unrecognizable by transformation into mosques, but the true glory of this zenith of Byzantine art is preserved in the mosaics of Hagia Sophia, which mostly date from the 9th to the 13th centuries, and above all in the interior of the **Chora Church** (Kariye Müzesi; see pp. 98–99), which is one of the wonders of the city.

The Inevitable Decline

While art flourished, however, the Empire's military fortunes did not. After a period of strength under the Macedonian dynasty (867–1081), the Byzantines came under pressure from Muslim Turks advancing from Asia. But their downfall was precipitated by their fellow Christians from the West. From 1099 the Crusades brought armies from Western Europe to the eastern Mediterranean. In principle these should have aided the Byzantines against their Muslim enemies, but in practice no love was lost between Catholic Christians who saw the Pope in Rome as the head of their religion and the Orthodox Christians of Constantinople.

In 1204, the warriors of the Fourth Crusade decided that the wealth of the city was more tempting than fighting Islam. They sacked Constantinople and carried off a vast booty. The Byzantine Empire never recovered from the shock. It limped on in a depleted state until finally conquered by the Ottoman Turks in 1453 (see pp. 66–69). Once the world's largest Christian power, the Byzantine Empire vanished from the face of the Earth.

Ottoman Museums

Ottoman culture abounds at every mosque and museum in Istanbul, not least amid the elaborate holy relics inside the Topkapı Palace (Topkapı Sarayı; see pp. 62–65). Turkish history is represented in full in a handful of galleries and museums that are off the beaten track.

■ PANORAMA 1453

Situated in the Topkapı Cultural Park in the Southern Golden Horn area, Panorama 1453 (Panorama Tarihi Müzesi) details the preparation, attack, and inundation of Constantinople by the Ottoman Turks in that same year. Vast canvases hung in chronological order allow visitors to take a stroll through the historic events as they unfolded. Perfectly placed, the site is a short walk from where the city walls were breached 550 years ago.

Topkapı Kültür Parkı • tel 0212 415 1453 • Closed Mon. • $ • Metro: Topkapı

■ MUSEUM OF TURKISH & ISLAMIC ART

On entering the Museum of Turkish & Islamic Art (Türk ve İslam Eserleri Müzesi) in the Old City neighborhood, you'll see original bleachers from the Hippodrome (see p. 70). Spectators watched charioteers racing through the square from these seats. Head upstairs and out onto a vast terrace overlooking the **Blue Mosque** (Sultan Ahmet Camii; see p. 54–55). A metal stairway leads up to a modern hangar filled with Ottoman-era art—including poetry written on parchment by the sultans and coffee-colored rugs from Uşak. In the older part of the building—once the palace chambers of İbrahim Paşa, Sultan Süleyman the Magnificent's grand vizier—you'll find a holy relics section, complete with a vial containing part of what is said to be Prophet Mohammed's beard.

At Meydanı Sokak 46 • tel 0212 518 1805 • Closed Mon. • $$ • Tram: Sultanahmet

■ VAKIFLAR CARPET MUSEUM

Housed inside the former soup kitchen of the Hagia Sophia (Ayasofya Müzesi; see pp. 60–61) in the Old City neighborhood, the Vakıflar Carpet

Turkish carpets hang in the Great Ceremonial Hall at the Museum of Turkish & Islamic Art.

Museum (Vakıflar Halı Müzesi) is arranged in three galleries. The first showcases the oldest carpets. Notice the Holbein portrait of British nobles chatting in front of a Turkish carpet at London's Somerset House. The second gallery displays Ottoman-era carpets from Anatolia, while the grandest prayer room carpets from Uşak line the walls of gallery three. At the far side of the room you'll see the wood-fired oven that once baked bread for the poor.

Soğukçeşme Sokağı • tel 0212 512 6993 • Closed Mon. • $$ • Tram: Sultanahmet • halimuzesi.com

■ TILE PAVILION

The handsome, 15th-century Tile Pavilion (Çinili Köşk Müzesi) —one of Istanbul's oldest surviving buildings—is part of a much larger range of exhibits held at the **Istanbul Archaeology Museums** (İstanbul Arkeoloji Müzeleri; see pp. 58–59). Tour the galleries for an overview of Turkey's ceramics history, with examples of the finest wares from Kütahya, İznik, and Selçuk.

Osman Hamdi Bey Yokuşu Sokak • tel 0212 520 7740 • Closed Mon. • $$ • Tram: Gülhane • istanbularkeoloji.gov.tr

Galata & Karaköy

Currently the city's two hippest neighborhoods, Galata and Karaköy skirt the southernmost edge of Beyoğlu in European Istanbul. Anchored by the gleaming contemporary art museums of SALT Galata and Istanbul Modern, the streets here have been gentrified with numerous popup bazaars, trendy artisans' ateliers, and chic boutiques. Galata's steady rise has occurred over the past half-dozen years or so, yet it is only since 2013 that Istanbul's cool kids have turned their attention to the former warehouse district of Karaköy. Make no mistake—fashionable as they may be, part of the attraction here is the fact that these neighborhoods remain a little raw around the edges. Turn a corner and you're likely to stumble upon a block of hardware stores, a no-frills workers' restaurant, or a historic site like the Yeraltı Mosque. It is this variety that guarantees visitors to Galata and Karaköy a truly diverse experience.

◄ **Hand-roasted
caffe lattes and
vegan brunches are
commonplace in
Karaköy's latest wave of
trendy sidewalk cafés.**

GALATA & KARAKÖY

Galata & Karaköy

Immerse yourself in homegrown culture, from whirling dervishes and nargile cafés to the finest contemporary art the city has to offer.

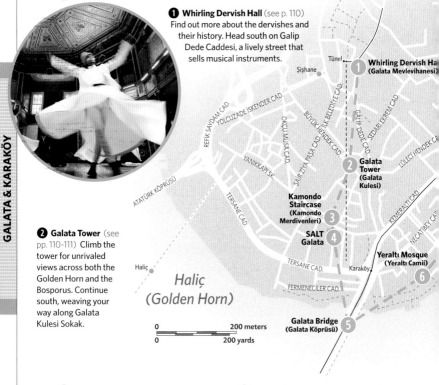

1 Whirling Dervish Hall (see p. 110) Find out more about the dervishes and their history. Head south on Galip Dede Caddesi, a lively street that sells musical instruments.

2 Galata Tower (see pp. 110-111) Climb the tower for unrivaled views across both the Golden Horn and the Bosporus. Continue south, weaving your way along Galata Kulesi Sokak.

3 Kamondo Staircase (see pp. 111-112) Admire the rippling shape of this art nouveau staircase. Cross Bankalar Caddesi, with its rococo bank headquarters, and walk one block east.

4 SALT Galata (see pp. 112-113) Opt for contemporary art or Ottoman banking history—or both—before walking east on Bankalar Caddesi, then south on Kemeraltı Caddesi to the Golden Horn.

GALATA & KARAKÖY DISTANCE: 3 MILES (5 KM) TIME: APPROX. 8 HOURS   METRO START: TÜNEL

8 Istanbul Modern (see pp. 116-117) Brush up on 20th-century Turkish art at this cutting-edge gallery on the dockside.

Nusretiye Mosque
(Nusretiye Camii)

Tophane

Kılıç Ali
Pasha Mosque
(Kılıç Ali
Paşa Camii)

TOPHANE

8 Istanbul Modern

7 Tophane

*Boğaziçi
(Bosporus)*

7 Tophane (see pp. 114-115) Soak up the atmosphere at one of many *nargile* waterpipe cafés. Stroll east on Meclis-i Mebusan Caddesi.

6 Yeraltı Mosque (see p. 114) Explore the city's only underground place of worship. Meander Karaköy's lively backstreets, heading east on Necatibey, Mumhane, or Kemankeş Caddesi.

5 Galata Bridge (see pp. 113-114) Stroll on both levels of this bustling bridge, then backtrack along Kemeraltı Caddesi, veering east onto Gümrük Sokak, and then south on Karantina Sokak.

GALATA & KARAKÖY

SAVVY **TRAVELER**

A whirling *sema* **ceremony** is a moving sight. There's a weekly performance at Whirling Dervish Hall *(Sun., 5 p.m., $$$$)*. Tickets go on sale at the museum gate on the morning of the event. Get there early—performances almost always sell out. If you can't make it, the Galata Mevlevileri also perform at the **Hodjapasha Culture Center** *(Ankara Caddesi, Hocapaşa Hamam Sokak 5–9D, tel 0212 511 4626, $$$$, hodjapasha .com)* near **Sirkeci Train Station** (see p. 77). Ceremonies are held here on most evenings, but check the website for details, as days and times vary.

Whirling Dervish Hall

1 The Whirling Dervish Hall (Galata Mevlevihanesi) was founded in 1491 as a religious center for dervishes (*mevlevi*)—adherents of the Sufi Muslim faith who seek spiritual union with God through a whirling dance called *sema*. Today the complex is a museum dedicated to the history of the Mevlevi Order. Shaded by fragrant lemon and grapefruit trees, the museum courtyard is dotted with tombstones, among them (on the left-hand side as you approach) that of the 17th-century spiritual leader and poet, Galip Dede. The gardens are also guarded by a family of friendly street cats. The highlight of the museum is the stunningly renovated, octagonal dancing room (*semahane*) in which live dervish ceremonies take place every Sunday evening. Other rooms at the center focus on different aspects of the religion, from worship through literature or music to culinary traditions. You'll also see a display of the hats and gowns used during the live performances and can watch a 3D video of a single dervish whirling.

Galip Dede Caddesi 15 • tel 0212 245 4141 • Closed Mon. • $ • Nostalgic Tram: Tünel • galatamevlevihanesimuzesi.gov.tr

Galata Tower

2 At 200 feet (61 m) tall, the Galata Tower (Galata Kulesi) is undoubtedly this neighborhood's landmark sight. Constructed by Genoese immigrants in 1348, the tower originally formed part of the city's defenses. Since that time, it has been used for various purposes, from a fire lookout point to its current incarnation as a panoramic viewing platform. Ride the elevator up to the seventh floor, then climb the remaining two sets of stairs to the tower's slim, 360-degree balcony. From here, enjoy the sublime views that stretch from the **Topkapı Palace** (Topkapı Sarayı; see pp. 62–65) and **Blue Mosque** (Sultan Ahmet Camii; see pp. 54–55) across the Bosporus to Asia. To feast your eyes on the views a little longer, stop for a glass of Turkish tea in the top-floor **Galata Tower Restaurant** *(tel 0212 293 8183)*. Alternatively, the cafés beneath the tower offer freshly pressed orange juice and snacks.

Büyük Hendek Sokak 2 • tel 0212 293 8180 • $ • Nostalgic Tram: Tünel; Tram: Karaköy

Kamondo Staircase

3 Nestled into Galata's backstreets, the art nouveau Kamondo Staircase (Kamondo Merdivenleri) was commissioned by wealthy Jewish banker Abraham Kamondo in 1860. Legend has it that Kamondo devised the steps' curved, almost braided shape to prevent his children from tumbling down the steep incline to

The ornate twists and turns of the Kamondo Staircase

Bankalar Caddesi (Banks Avenue) below. View the staircase's undulating form from the top and see if you agree. Then read the display boards attached to the staircase for a formal history of its construction. The staircase has long been a favorite with photographers, most notably the French photographer, Henri Cartier-Bresson, who took an iconic shot here in 1964.

Kart Çınar Sokak/Bankalar Caddesi • Tram: Karaköy

SALT Galata

Housed in the former headquarters of the Ottoman National Bank, SALT Galata is a nonprofit space dedicated to contemporary culture. Stroll through the polished wooden doors into the building's marble-covered interior. To the right, the magnificent friezes high on the wall are reminders of this venue's money-fueled past. To the left, you'll see a glass-fronted public

The impressive triple-height space at the heart of SALT Galata

GALATA & KARAKÖY

research library containing thousands of history books on Istanbul. Straight ahead, the restaurant **Neolokal** *(tel 0212 244 0016, closed Mon., $$$$, neolokal.com)* has been earning accolades since opening in late 2014. Opposite the restaurant, the **Robinson Crusoe 389** international bookshop *(tel 0212 245 5439, closed Mon., rob389.com)* sells Istanbul design and photography books. SALT hosts an impressive calendar of temporary exhibitions, normally held on one of the subterranean levels. Artworks may range from cutting-edge video to photography. Check the website for upcoming events.

Also on the premises, the **Ottoman Bank Museum** (Osmanlı Bankası Müzesi; *tel 0212 334 2200, closed Mon., obmuze.com)* chronicles the ups and downs of the late Ottoman Empire via sample banknotes, shares certificates, and personal letters from the Sultans. It's far more fun that it sounds, especially when you learn that the Empire's last rulers used the institution as a personal piggy bank.

Bankalar Caddesi 11 • tel 0212 334 2200 • Closed Mon. • Tram: Karaköy
• saltonline.org

Galata Bridge

5 The Galata Bridge (Galata Köprüsü) spans the mouth of the Golden Horn estuary (*Haliç* in Turkish) and links the neighborhoods of Eminönü and **Sultanahmet** (see pp. 50–65) with the European zones of Galata and Karaköy. The upper level of the bridge is a flurry of activity, with cars, taxis, and the tramway vying for space. Stroll the large sidewalks lined with enthusiastic local fishermen that flank the road, then loop back along the lower level. Here restaurants and bars occupy both sides of the bridge—brace

GOOD **EATS**

■ KARAKÖY ÖZSÜT

This family-run eatery serves *kaymak* (clotted cream) made from milk sourced from their own herd of water buffalo with honey and bread. Thick soups and other savory bites also feature. **Yemişçi Hasan Sokak 9/11, tel 0212 293 3031, $**

■ LOKANTA MAYA

Michelin-star-trained Aegean chef Didem Şenol draws locals with her pomegranate-flecked spinach salad and Black Sea anchovies *(hamsi)*. **Kemankeş Caddesi 35A, tel 0212 252 6884, $$$**

■ NAIF

This popular Karaköy spot offers modern Turkish dishes that may include homemade ravioli stuffed with chicken and walnuts *(mantı)*. **Mumhane Caddesi 52, tel 0212 251 5335, $$**

GALATA & KARAKÖY

yourself to ignore the owners' calls if you're not in the mood. But if you do stop for a meal or drink, you can take in the vistas over the city's Asian shores to the east, and the Golden Horn to the west.

Kemeraltı Caddesi • Tram: Karaköy

Yeraltı Mosque

6 Originally a Byzantine prison, then a military arsenal, today the Yeraltı Mosque (Yeraltı Camii) is a subterranean place of worship—*yeraltı* translates as underground. On entering at street level, descend the mosque's short set of stairs. Once inside, you'll notice that—unlike other mosques, where worship normally takes place in a large, open room—the vaulted space here is divided into individual prayer nooks separated by chunky rectangular columns. The effect is to create a warren-like series of dimly lit passages. Head toward the rear of the mosque to see—bathed in an eerie green light—the glass-encased tombs of two martyrs killed during the seventh-century Arab siege of Constantinople.

Kemankeş Caddesi • Closed Fri. and during prayer times • Tram: Karaköy

Tophane

7 Along the banks of the Bosporus, the suburb of Tophane is experiencing a period of intense regeneration. First the Kılıç Ali Pasha Mosque and hamam complex, and now the ornate 19th-century **Nusretiye Mosque** (Nusretiye Camii) have undergone extensive renovation. Both are seriously impressive architecturally, the former having been the work of Mimar Sinan and the latter of Armenian architect Krikor Balyan, the first of five generations of Ottoman architects to shape the Istanbul skyline. Walking between the two mosques, you can't

IN **THE KNOW**

During Byzantine times, when the city was besieged, the Golden Horn was closed off with a heavy chain, to prevent enemy boats from entering these waters. On the northern side, the chain is said to have been fixed to the ancient building that is now Yeraltı Mosque.

Relaxing over a game of backgammon at a *nargile* bar in Tophane

miss the huge, 18th-century **Tophane Fountain,** with its elaborately carved surfaces. Join the locals in one of the adjacent cafés, such as popular **Nargilem Café** (see p. 140), for a water pipe, a glass of apple tea, and a round of backgammon. Walk on to visit any number of the neighborhood's art galleries (see also pp. 122–123). Favorites include industrial **Mixer** (see p. 122); workshop and exhibition space **Studio-X** (*Meclis-i Mebusan Caddesi 35A, tel 0212 292 0747, closed Mon. and Sun.*); and **Krampf Gallery** (*Kemeraltı Caddesi 41, tel 0212 293 9314*), showcasing international artists.

Kemeraltı Caddesi • Tram: Tophane

Istanbul Modern

8 See pp. 116–117.

Meclis-i Mebusan Caddesi • tel 0212 334 7300 • Closed Mon. and Jan. 1 • $$ (audio guide $) • Tram: Tophane • istanbulmodern.org

Istanbul Modern

A hundred years of Turkish art in one of the city's most innovative spaces.

GALATA & KARAKÖY

Children are introduced to contemporary Turkish art at Istanbul Modern.

Housed in a converted 1950s cargo warehouse on the banks of the Bosporus in Tophane, this outstanding gallery ranks as Istanbul's finest modern art venue. When the gallery opened in 2004, it was the first time that such a substantial collection of 20th-century Turkish art had ever gone on display in the city. Tour its impressive halls for a comprehensive insight into modern Turkey's art history and make use of the interactive iPads dotted around the place to learn more about those exhibits that most catch your eye.

■ A CENTURY OF TURKISH ART

The main floor of the gallery houses **Past and Present,** a permanent exhibition featuring Turkish art of the 20th century. Around 200 works from the museum's collection are on show at any one time, grouped chronologically. Look for Turkish interpretations of the major modern art movements— Impressionist works by **İbrahim Çallı** and cubist and constructivist pieces by **Nurullah Berk** and **Bedri Rahmi Eyüboğlu.** Later works by **Burhan Doğançay, Ömer Uluç,** and **Adnan Çoker** among others take inspiration from Islamic art and architecture.

■ VISIONARY CREATIONS

Showcased artworks become increasingly critical and political from the 1970s onward. The video **"Headless Woman or the Belly Dance"** by Nil Yalter plays on a loop in a small alcove. This feminist film, portraying the artist's stomach as she pens a poem on it and dances, was the first piece of video art exhibited in Turkey. In a nearby viewing room, Kutluğ Ataman's documentary **"Women Who Wear Wigs"** is equally avant-garde.

SAVVY **TRAVELER**

Short on time? Stop in the vast foyer to pick up a 45-minute audio guide for a tour of the gallery's highlights. Pause for a moment to admire the floor-to-ceiling Bosporus vistas. If you plan to take things a little more slowly, the **Istanbul Modern Restaurant** (tel 0212 292 2612, closed Mon., $$) is located here, too, and has its own sunny waterside terrace.

■ FLEETING FUN

Take the dramatic glass and metal-chain staircase to the museum's lower level. (The staircase, entitled **"Stairway to Hell,"** is an artwork in its own right, by Italian artist Monica Bonvicini.) This lower floor houses an art-house cinema that shows international films, as well as three temporary exhibition spaces. Of these, one is always dedicated to photography—recent exhibitions have featured images from Magnum's extensive archives.

There's also a library down here and, alongside it, British artist Richard Wentworth's intriguing **"False Ceiling."** This permanent installation consists of several hundred books— from both the East and the West— suspended from the ceiling.

GALATA & KARAKÖY

Meclis-i Mebusan Caddesi • tel 0212 334 7300 • Closed Mon. and Jan. 1 • $$ (audio guide $) • Tram: Tophane • istanbulmodern.org

Turkish Fare

Turkish food is locally sourced and highly seasonal. The freshest ingredients are gathered from Turkey's vast landscape, from fertile fields in the east, to hilltop orchards in the west, and thousands of miles of coastline that encompass the Black Sea, Aegean Sea, and Mediterranean. Whether opting for lunch in a workers' restaurant or an upscale meal of sharing *meze* platters, epicurean visitors are in for a treat in Istanbul.

GALATA & KARAKÖY

Asitane Restaurant's Helatiye—a traditional Ottoman dessert made from almonds, sugar, and butter
Opposite: A typical Turkish breakfast

Ottoman Foundations

For many centuries, Ottoman chefs took inspiration from all corners of the land—borders that enveloped North Africa, Eastern Europe, and all of the Middle East. At the empire's peak, more than 1,000 chefs whipped up exotic delicacies for the sultan and his family in the enormous **Topkapı Palace** (Topkapı Sarayı; see pp. 62–65) kitchens. Top Istanbul spots to sample these ancient recipes today include **Asitane Restaurant** (see p. 97) in Edirnekapı (Southern Golden Horn neighborhood), and **Feriye Lokantası** (*Çırağan Caddesi 40, tel 0212 227 2216, $$–$$$, feriye.com*) in Ortaköy (Bosporus & Nişantaşi neighborhood).

Breakfast of Champions

For the majority of Turks, the morning meal is little less than a feast. A traditional Turkish breakfast (*kahvaltı*) will always feature a selection of local cheeses, tomato and cucumber salad, olives, bread, homemade jams, pastries, and tea.

The spread will usually also include scrambled eggs mixed with chopped tomatoes and bell peppers *(menemen)* and clotted-cream-style *kaymak* (which is made from water buffalos' milk).

Meyhane Meals

Throughout Istanbul, lively evening meals are dished up in the city's backstreet taverns *(meyhanes)*. These unpretentious restaurants offer dinners comprising three components: sharing dishes similar to tapas *(meze)*, fish *(balık)*, and Turkey's strong anise-flavored alcohol, usually diluted with water *(rakı)*. There are rarely menus. Instead, you'll be shown the day's myriad of specials—such as samphire sautéed with garlic or octopus salad—simply point and pick. Expect tasty eats, boisterous crowds, and an entertaining

BEST **BREAKFASTS**

While a full breakfast will almost always be included with your hotel room, seek out the following for something special:

Van Kahvaltı Evi in Beyoğlu, which serves southeastern Turkish-style breakfasts of herby cheeses and potato pancakes *(gözleme)*. **Defterdar Yokuşu 52, tel 0212 249 6924, $**

Café Privato in Galata, whose equally enticing honeyed fritters and generous glasses of pomegranate juice lure the locals. **Galip Dede Caddesi 3, tel 0212 293 205, $**

GALATA & KARAKÖY

**Hassa Böreği—a traditional
pastry dish stuffed with cheese,
green olives, walnuts, yogurt,
green onions, and tarragon
Opposite: Cihangir's Asri
Turşucu—every neighborhood
has a resident pickle maker.**

atmosphere at **Asmalı Cavit** (*Asmalımescit Caddesi 16/D, tel 0212 292 4950, $$*) and **Çukur Meyhane** (*Kartal Sokak, tel 0212 244 5575, $$*), both in the Beyoğlu neighborhood.

Regional Recipes

The trendiest Turkish cuisine focuses on strong regional flavors. You'll see fresh seafood and wild herbs from the Aegean coastline, or more typical Middle Eastern dishes, such as hummus from southeastern Hatay province. Other favorites include lamb served with a smoky eggplant purée (*hünkar beğendi*) and eggplant stuffed with tomatoes, onions, and herbs (*imam bayıldı*). Often the most authentic place to taste these local specialties is in a no-frills, canteen-style workers' restaurant (*esnaf lokantası*). You'll find two in the Beyoğlu neighborhoood: Try **Hayvore** (*Turnacıbaşı Sokak 4, tel 0212 245 7501, $*) for anchovies, buttery beans, and cornbread from the Black Sea, or head to **Özkonak** (*Akarsu Yokuşu Caddesi 46/B, tel 0212 249 1307, $*) for Anatolian ravioli (*mantı*). Take note—many of these restaurants are cash only.

Daily Drinks

Turkey boasts the highest per capita consumption of tea (*çay*) in the world, and everywhere you go in Istanbul, you'll see tea boys of all ages carrying trays of tea-filled glasses to locals. They drink it black with plenty of sugar. Tea only gained such popularity relatively recently, however. At the height of the Ottoman Empire, coffee was the hot beverage of choice. Turkish coffee is always served black, and sugar must be requested before brewing. It's a short drink—similar in size to an Italian espresso—and the grounds settle at the bottom of the cup. Other popular Turkish drinks include thin, salted yogurt *(ayran)*; pickled red carrot and turnip juice *(şalgam)*; a sweet drink made from orchid roots that is served hot during wintertime *(salep)*; and the local anise-flavored firewater *(rakı)*. There are also countless fresh fruit juice vendors throughout the city, their carts stacked high with piles of oranges and pomegranates.

A Sweet Tooth

Turkish desserts range from the seriously sweet sheets of filo pastry layered with pistachios, melted butter, and sugar syrup *(baklava)* to creamy, comforting puddings, such as rice pudding made using water buffalo milk, baked, and topped with cinnamon *(sütlaç)* or a mix that combines wheat, beans, dried fruits, and nuts *(aşure)*. If visiting during the colder months, be sure to sample the popular candied pumpkin dessert *(kabak tatlısı)*.

Gallery Hopping

Istanbul Modern kick-started a now thriving, modern art scene. Established galleries have seen a welcome renaissance and new ones are springing up in former factories and warehouses. Today, galleries are scattered all over Istanbul, while Tophane and Beyoğlu have become art hubs in their own right.

■ MIXER

Mixer, at the northern end of the Karaköy neighborhood, could be in New York's Lower East Side or Shoreditch in East London—its name splattered in yellow on a cool gray facade certainly makes for an arresting entrance. Calling itself an art space rather than gallery, Mixer's goal is to support the production of sustainable art and not simply to sell. Expect underground art by young Turkish artists working across all disciplines.

Boğazkesen Caddesi 45 • tel 0212 243 5443 • Closed Mon. • Tram: Tophane • mixerarts.com

■ RODEO

If you want to see bold and inventively curated conceptual shows of local and regional artists, Beyoğlu's Rodeo is the place. Gallery owner Sylvia Kouvali was in her mid-20s when she opened her space in a former tobacco factory in Tophane in 2007. She moved to the current space in 2012. Transforming an apartment into a hip space is no mean feat, but Kouvali has managed to do just that, to huge commercial and critical success. Hers is one of only two Istanbul galleries that have also opened a branch in London.

Sıraselviler Caddesi 49/1 • tel 0212 293 5800 • Closed Mon.–Wed., Sun. • Metro: Taksim • rodeo-gallery.com

■ GALERI NEV

In a Beyoğlu building stuffed with galleries, Galeri Nev is surely the frontrunner. Exhibitions showcase artists—mostly locals—who regularly make waves at international art fairs. Check out the works of video artist Ali Kazma and those of İnci Eviner, known for her ink illustrations.

İstiklal Cadessi, Mısır Apartment 163 • tel 0212 252 1525 • Closed Mon. and Sun. • Metro: Taksim • galerinevistanbul.com

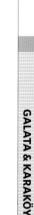

Attending a Turkish contemporay art exhibition at Galeri Nev

■ GALERIST

Next door to the **Pera Museum** (see p. 132) in Beyoğlu, this impressive gallery is home to works by Nil Yalter, a pioneer in the 1970s French feminist movement; Cypriot-born Hussein Chalayan known for gravity-defying haute couture; and avant-garde Young British Artist Gavin Turk. The gallery also represents the late Semiha Berksoy, Turkey's first opera singer, who also left a significant imprint on the country's visual arts scene.

Meşrutiyet Caddesi 67 • tel 0212 252 1896 • Closed Mon. and Sun. • Metro: Şişhane • galerist.com.tr

■ MILLÎ REASÜRANS ART GALLERY

A Nişantaşı neighborhood veteran, this gallery has hosted more than 150 exhibitions in its 20-year history. Favoring architecture as a theme and photography as a medium, the gallery's standout shows include an exhibition focusing on Mimar Sinan's masterpieces, atmospheric landscapes by Turkey's celebrated filmmaker Nuri Bilge Ceylan, and black-and-white images by the Spanish surrealist photographer Chema Madoz.

Maçka Caddesi 35 • tel: 0212 230 1976 • Closed Mon. and Sun. • Metro: Osmanbey • millireasuranssanatgalerisi.com

The Heart of Beyoğlu

Istanbul's cultural, entertainment, and hard-partying center, the district of Beyoğlu offers the same Europeanized selection of cafés, stores, churches, and clubs as it did centuries ago, when the Venetians and Dutch and, later, French and British headquartered their ambassadors in this Italianate quarter. The legacy of European largesse lives on in the belle époque splendor of many of the district's buildings; few are more handsome than the Pera Palace Hotel. While nothing shouts Beyoğlu quite like İstiklal Caddesi—the broad boulevard that sweeps through its heart, all restaurants, malls, theaters, and bars—Beyoğlu's formerly gritty backstreets are now laced with vintage stores, welcoming hamams, and eclectic galleries and museums.

◐ **A Nostalgic Tram ferries locals and tourists the length of İstiklal Caddesi, the district's main thoroughfare.**

The Heart of Beyoğlu

*Grand-scale streets with piazzas, malls, and markets—
this is Istanbul at its most European.*

❼ Fish Market (see p. 132) Explore the Fish Market's north and south quarters. Return to İstiklal Caddesi and walk south to Kallavi Sokak, then west onto Meşrutiyet Caddesi. Continue south.

❽ Pera Museum (see p. 132) Explore all four floors of this private art collection. Walk south a few steps.

❾ Pera Palace Hotel (see p. 133) Visit Room 101, once Atatürk's room and now a small museum. Return once more to İstiklal Caddesi. Walk south to Tünel, the last building on the street.

❿ Tünel (see p. 133) Seek out a bar in the Asmalı Mescit area for some live music and a reviving drink.

**BEYOĞLU   DISTANCE: 2.5 MILES (4 KM)
TIME: APPROX. 9 HOURS   METRO START: TAKSIM**

GEZİ PARKI

Taksim

Taksim Square
(Taksim Meydanı)

Cihangir

CİHANGİR

İstanbul Boğazı
(Bosporus)

0		400 meters
0		400 yards

MECLİS-İ MEBUSAN CAD.

1 Taksim Square (see p. 128) Admire the 36-foot-tall (11 m) Monument of the Republic at the center of the square. Make your way to the square's western corner.

2 İstiklal Caddesi (see pp. 134-135) Explore this bustling avenue before returning to the street's only mosque, the Hüseyin Ağa Camii. Turn into Sadri Alışık Sokak opposite, and head south.

3 Cihangir (see pp. 128-129) Drift past alfresco cafés and one-off boutiques, stopping for a drink or some gourmet shopping. From the Firüzağa Mosque, walk west on Palaska Sokak, then south on Hüseyin Ağa Bahçe Sokak.

THE HEART OF BEYOĞLU

6 Flower Market (see p. 131) Admire the floral decoration at the entrance to this covered passageway. Leave through the mall's upper exit and enter the pedestrian-only fish market.

5 Çukurcuma (see pp. 130-131) Shop for antiques and vintage clothing in the streets around Faik Paşa Caddesi before heading north on Turnacıbaşı Caddesi. Head west on İstiklal Caddesi.

4 Museum of Innocence (see pp. 129-130) See how Orhan Pamuk's creative displays mirror events in his eponymous novel. Retrace your steps on Hüseyin Ağa Bahçe Sokak, veering west into Çukurcuma Caddesi.

Taksim Square

1 Taksim Square (Taksim Meydanı) is Istanbul's answer to New York's Times Square or London's Trafalgar Square. Out-of-towners come here to pose for photographs with age-old city trams in the background. The name Taksim is derived from the Ottoman-era, octagonal, stone reservoir building near the tram terminus on the west side of the square. Now the **Republic Art Gallery** (Taksim Cumhuriyet Sanat Galerisi; *İstiklal Caddesi 2, tel 0212 245 7832),* the building hosts temporary exhibitions on Istanbul's cultural history. At the square's center stands the **Monument of the Republic** (Cumhuriyet Anıtı), commissioned by Atatürk and unveiled in 1928. This soldier-statesman founded modern Turkey in 1923, after the fall of the Ottoman Empire. Circle the monument to see, on its north face, a depiction of Atatürk in his role as a military commander, and on its south face, Atatürk dressed in Western clothing, symbolizing his role as a modern statesman. On the sidewalk nearby, you'll see *simit* sellers (see p. 87) hawking their sesame seed bread rolls. Turn to face **Taksim Park** (Taksim Gezi Parkı) to the north. Peaceful demonstrations for work, human, or gay rights often commence here.

Taksim Meydanı • Metro: Taksim

IN **THE KNOW**

Look closely, and all over Istanbul you'll see birdhouses attached to the facades of many prominent buildings. Made from stone, they range from the simplest boxes to ornate, miniature pavilions and palaces. These birdhouses appear on all types of buildings and were a key architectural feature throughout the Ottoman Empire. See if you can spot the one gracing the exterior of the **Information Center** in Taksim Square.

İstiklal Caddesi

2 See pp. 134–135.

İstiklal Caddesi • Metro: Taksim

Cihangir

3 Cihangir is easily Istanbul's most liberal and charming neighborhood. The **Ağa Hamam** (Ağa Hamamı; *Turnacıbaşı Caddesi 48, tel 0212 249 5027, $$$$, agahamami.com)* is a case in

THE HEART OF BEYOĞLU

point. Built in 1562, this Turkish bath, located where Turnacıbaşı Caddesi intersects with Sadri Alışık Sokak, offers mixed-sex bathing. The atmosphere here is convivially historic, although standards (and prices) may be lower than in the tourist-centric steam baths of Sultanahmet. Wander the streets east of the baths, dotted as they are with antique shops and hip bars. Explore upmarket Turkish food and wine stores like **La Cave** (*Sıraselviler Caddesi 109, tel 0212 243 2405, lacavesarap.com*) and the **Kilye/Suvla Shop** (*Lenger Sokak 2, tel 0212 245 5634*). Stop at **1 Kahve** (*Bakraç Sokak 19–1, $*) for a glass of mint lemonade. Sit outside on the leafy street corner. Before leaving the neighborhood, be sure to see the mint green **Firüzağa Mosque** (*Firüzağa Camii; Palaska Sokak*).

Intersection of Taktaki Yokuşu & Defterdar Yokuşu
• Metro: Taksim

Museum of Innocence

4 Orhan Pamuk's Museum of Innocence (Masumiyet Müzesi), based upon his eponymous novel, is a treasure trove of Turkish upper-class kitsch from the 1970s. In the novel, wealthy Istanbullu Kemal falls in love with an impoverished distant cousin, Füsun. Over the course of the tormented romance that ensues, Kemal collects "memories" from her home, among them the 4,213 cigarette butts exhibited on the first floor of the museum. Each of the

Box 58 at the Museum of Innocence is "Tombala," which features a popular game played by families at New Year.

four stories of this former Çukurcuma family home houses display cabinets filled with vintage objets d'art—a cabinet for each of the book's 83 chapters. In **Kissing on the Lips** (Box 12), you'll see numerous picture cards of famous soccer players and film stars, suspended on wires. **The Dogs** (Box 65) is filled with a collection of miniature dog figurines. Pamuk spent years collecting these items to inspire his writing as he authored his semi-fictional account of 1970s Istanbul high society.

Dalgıç Çıkmazı 2 • tel 0212 252 9738 • Closed Mon. and Jan. 1 • $$$ • Metro: Taksim • masumiyetmuzesi.org

Çukurcuma

5 If you liked the exhibits displayed in the award-winning **Museum of Innocence** (see above), you'll love the antique stores that line Çukurcuma's backstreets—more so, because you can

THE HEART OF BEYOĞLU

Barrows laden with bric-a-brac are a common sight in the backstreets of Çukurcuma.

buy the goods on display here. This atmospheric district occupies a little pocket of streets south of Turnacıbaşı Caddesi and west of Ağa Hamamı Sokak. Lose yourself amid the teashops, furniture restoration factories, vintage fashion stores, and fruit vendors as you make your way uphill to **İstiklal Caddesi** (see pp. 134–135). The little green **Çukurcuma Mosque** (Çukurcuma Camii; *Çukurcuma Caddesi 41*) is typical of the quarter's wooden clapboard architecture. The buildings become bolder and antiques stores more upscale as you head north on Faik Paşa Caddesi toward Turnacıbaşı Caddesi. Try **Objects of Desire** (*Faik Paşa Caddesi 6*) for 1970s bikes, games, and plastic telephones, and **Deform Records** (*Turnacıbaşı Caddesi 45*) for 1960s Turkish and international funk and soul. The **Galatasaray Hamam** (Galatasaray Hamamı; see p. 28) is a friendly neighborhood steam bath.

Faik Paşa Caddesi and Turnacıbaşı Caddesi • Nostalgic Tram: Galatasaray

GOOD **EATS**

■ DATLI MAYA

This hole-in-the-wall Çukurcuma eatery is open from breakfast until dusk, serving cuisine based around a single wood-fired oven. Try the local *pide* pizza with anchovy and pomegranate salad. **Türkgücü Caddesi 59/A, tel 0216 292 9057, $**

■ FICCIN

This classic business lunch spot occupies several premises on Beyoğlu's Kallavi Sokak. Try the yogurt soup and pickled red mullet. **Kallavi Sokak 1, tel 0212 243 8353, $**

■ MEZE BY LEMON TREE

Come here to eat *meze* with a contemporary twist—the seafood dishes are particularly exciting. Try whole octopus braised in butter with arugula. **Meşrutiyet Caddesi 83/B, tel 0212 252 8302, $$$**

Flower Market

6 As soon as you step into the Flower Market (Çiçek Pasajı) from **İstiklal Caddesi,** cast your eyes skyward. This Italianate indoor mall was once an opera house—as you may have guessed from the rarified surroundings and balconies—but was transformed into a flower market a century ago. Today, this "flower passage," as the name translates, is lined with seafood restaurants at which Istanbul's elite come to dine. Ignore the calls of the restaurateurs and concentrate, instead, on the marble balconies and chandeliers—you'll get a far better lunch in the nearby **Fish Market** (Balık Pazarı; see p. 132).

Sait Paşa Geçidi 176/6 • Nostalgic Tram: Galatasaray

Fish Market

7 Vibrant and colorful, Beyoğlu's Fish Market (Balık Pazarı) is a feast for the senses. Stalls are laden with the freshest Aegean lobster (*ıstakoz*), Black Sea turbot (*kalkan*), and Mediterranean sea bass (*levrek*)—the crimson gills of the fish are turned inside out to show how fresh they are. Vendors call out their deals of the day, while restaurateurs invite you to choose anything you like the look of for a simply cooked lunch. The aroma of beautifully cooked fish with fresh herbs and spices is enticing. Join local businessmen for an upmarket lunch at the **Mer Balık** (*Sahne Sokak 23, tel 0212 244 9797, $$$*) or snack on fish sandwiches (*balık ekmek*), fried mussel skewers (*midye tava*), and grilled squid (*kalamar ızgara*) at no-frills joints like **Özgün** (*Sahne Sokak 9, tel 0212 243 4247, $*).

Sahne Sokak and around • Nostalgic Tram: Galatasaray

Pera Museum

8 The best little museum in Istanbul packs an incredible punch. Take the elevator up to the Pera Museum's (Pera Müzesi) permanent **Ambassadors and Painters** exhibition. Collected by wealthy Turkish socialites Suna and İnan Kıraç over the last three decades or so, the scores of canvases here capture Istanbul through the ages by way of Ottoman portraits, Bosporus panoramas, and sultry hamam scenes. Make your way to the must-see *Tortoise Trainer* canvas on the same floor. Painted by late Ottoman artist (and founder of the **Istanbul Archaeology Museums;** İstanbul Arkeoloji Müzeleri; see pp. 58–59) Osman Hamdi Bey, it's worth many millions of dollars. Recent temporary exhibitions have included the works of Pablo Picasso, Frida Kahlo, and Henri Cartier-Bresson.

Meşrutiyet Caddesi 65 • tel 0212 334 9900 • Closed Mon. and Jan. 1 • $$$ • Nostalgic Tram: Odakule • peramuzesi.org.tr

SAVVY **TRAVELER**

When planning your visit to the Pera Museum, take advantage of **Young Wednesdays**—admission to the museum is free for students every Wednesday—and **Long Fridays,** when the museum stays open until 10 p.m.

Pera Palace Hotel

9 The venerable Pera Palace Hotel (Pera Palas Oteli) was built to host ritzy guests who stepped off the Orient Express from Paris. Stride through the double glass doors and past the liveried door staff. A century ago, elite travelers including American writer Ernest Hemingway and British Prime Minister Sir Winston Churchill would have found themselves in the **Orient Bar** to the right of the entrance hall. More authentically historic is the **Kubbeli Saloon** to the rear of the hotel. Spend an hour or so reclining on a velvet lounger over Turkish delight and Arabian coffee fit for a sultan.

Tepebaşı Çamlık Sokak 2, • tel 0212 337 4000 • Nostalgic Tram: Odakule • jumeirah .com

The Pera Palace Hotel was the first building in Istanbul to have an elevator.

Tünel

10 Tünel is two things. Firstly, it's the funicular that breezes downhill to the **Galata Bridge** (Galata Köprüsü; see pp. 113–114). Secondly, Tünel is the name of the hip area surrounding the Metro terminal. Impromptu concerts are held in front of the cafés along Galip Dede Caddesi. Composers practice their Ottoman-era instruments outside the area's music stores. And locals sell handmade cookies, backgammon sets, haute couture, tableware, and much else besides in the surrounding streets.

Intersection of İstiklal Caddesi and Galip Dede Caddesi • Metro: Şişhane/Tünel

İstiklal Caddesi

*Join the locals in a leisurely stroll on Istanbul's
pedestrian-only shopping boulevard.*

The handsome facade of the Flower Passage on İstiklal Caddesi

A century ago, İstiklal Caddesi was known as the Grand Rue de Péra. With
embassies of Britain, France, Russia, and Sweden lining the boulevard, it was
Istanbul's smartest avenue. Today, literally millions of locals come here daily
to promenade past İstiklal Caddesi's boutiques and bars, or to admire the
sights from within its vintage tram. Look up at the grand buildings that line
both sides of this former European colony. They range from beaux arts to
Renaissance to neoclassical in style.

■ STEEPLES & MINARETS

Mosques and modernism go side-by-side on historic İstiklal Caddesi. The **Hüseyin Ağa Mosque** (Hüseyin Ağa Camii) is marked by a minaret at the junction of Sadri Alışık Sokak. Soak up the atmosphere in its stone courtyard. The mosque dates from 1596, yet overlooks Istanbul's hippest design hotel, Mama Shelter, just next door. Italian, Greek, French, and Armenian communities built churches here by the dozen. The prettiest include redbrick **St. Anthony of Padua Church** (Sent Antuan Kilisesi; *No. 171*) recessed from the street, and the **Church of St. Mary Draperis** (Santa Maria Draperis; *No. 215*) accessed by a series of stone steps. Masses are still said in a number of different languages.

■ PASSAGE TO EUROPE

Several age-old indoor shopping malls (*pasaj*) lead off İstiklal Caddesi. Wander into any one of these to admire rococo ceilings and antique tiles that carry a sense of European splendor. Just north of the Galatasaray Nostalgic Tram stop, turn into **Avrupa Pasajı** for elegant 1950s watches and vintage jewelry. Gaze up at the neoclassical statues that line the roof, then browse the 30 or so stalls of secondhand books in the **Aslıhan Pasajı** next door. Nearby **Atlas Pasajı** hosts an old cinema and fashion outlets.

■ SMOKE & MIRRORS

Notice the neon-lit establishments perched high in the buildings above İstiklal Caddesi. Many advertise fortune telling (*fal*) and tobacco water pipes (*nargile*). Both are Turkish café staples in this bohemian quarter. If you're feeling adventurous, climb up the rickety stairs to try one or two. Alternatively, the cafés inside Hazzopulo and Suriye passages serve simple glasses of tea.

IN THE KNOW

Most of the grand embassies along İstiklal Caddesi have been converted into consulates. Many hold public events and photography shows inside their halls—in particular, the **Greek** (*No. 60*) and **Dutch** (*No. 197*) diplomatic missions. Most accessible of all is the **French Consulate** (*No. 4*), complete with a little-known café (open to the public) just behind the security gate. Revolving exhibitions at the adjoining gallery are superb.

İstiklal Caddesi • Metro: Taksim

Literary Istanbul

Countless writers have had a literary love affair with Istanbul. That's just as well—a city with a 2,000-year history requires voices from the past to bring it to life. From the Byzantine era through the Ottoman Empire years and into the 21st century, local writers and foreign visitors alike have sought to capture the very essence of this constantly evolving city through tales of love, war, imperial expansion, revolution, and the everyday.

Orhan Pamuk strolls the streets of Çukurcuma, the setting for his novel *The Museum of Innocence*. Opposite: Books are piled high at one of Istanbul's many secondhand bookstores.

Early Chronicles

Among some of the earliest surviving texts are *The Secret History* court letters of Procopius, ca A.D. 550, in which he gossips about his tyrannical boss (and builder of the **Hagia Sophia;** Ayasofya Müzesi; see pp. 60–61), Justinian. Later, eccentric explorer Evliya Çelebi traveled the Ottoman Empire. In his recently translated *Seyahatname* (*An Ottoman Traveler*), he describes 17th-century sites, such as Istanbul's Kürkçü Han silk trading hall, that are still in business today.

Foreign Invasion

The unruly crumble of the Ottoman Empire from the early 1800s onward attracted dreamers and dilettantes by the score. Frenchman Pierre Loti took Istanbul so much to heart that the city returned the favor. The suburb of Eyüp has a hill, a funicular cable car, and a panoramic café named after him (see pp. 97 and 156). In his 19th-century travel memoir *Constantinople,* Italian novelist

Edmondo de Amicis describes traffic on the **Galata Bridge** (Galata Köprüsü; see pp. 113–114): "one can see all of Constantinople go by... a Bedouin wrapped in a white mantle and a Turk in muslin turban and sky-blue kaftan... a dervish with his tall conical hat... who makes way for the carriage of a European ambassador." The same cosmopolitan scene is apparent today.

20th-Century Tales

In the 1960s and 1970s, author Yaşar Kemal weaved magical tales revolving around social justice, like *Memed, My Hawk*. Nobel Prize winner Orhan Pamuk sets his contemporary novels and memoirs around the chic suburbs of Nişantaşı (see p. 151) and Beyoğlu. His stories draw heavily on his 1970s and 1980s upper-class upbringing.

see pp. 113–114
see p. 151

FIVE BEST
ISTANBUL BOOKS

Aziyadé Pierre Loti (1879) Dramatic forbidden love between a French officer and a Turkish girl.

Bright Sun, Strong Tea Tom Brosnahan (2004) A lucid recollection of late 20th-century city life.

Deadly Web Barbara Nadel (2005) A crime novel featuring hard-drinking Inspector Çetin Ikmen.

Istanbul, Memories and the City Orhan Pamuk (2005) A warts-and-all history of Istanbul's elite.

The Bastard of Istanbul Elif Şafak (2006) Strong women abound in this feminist take on modern-day Turkey.

THE HEART OF BEYOĞLU

Nightlife

To sample Istanbul's nightlife could mean anything from watching a live belly-dancing show to hitting the dance floor yourself. Join an urban crowd sipping beer in Karaköy, relax for an hour or two with a *nargile* pipe in Tophane, or sit down to traditional Turkish fare in one of the city's many inns *(meyhanes)*.

■ BELLY DANCING

Belly dancing was introduced to Turkey from Egypt. Often more mesmerizing than exotic, the dancers play tiny cymbals as they gyrate around the room. No establishment is more professional than **Sultana's** *(Kahan 40, tel 0212 219 3904, $$$$, sultanas -nights.com)*, a three-minute walk from Taksim Square in the Beyoğlu neighborhood. Nightly shows *(from 9 p.m.–11:30 p.m.)* often star the peerless Didem, whose dances have garnered over 100 million YouTube views. She has even belly danced at a private birthday party of Madonna's. Performances include dinner, unlimited local drinks, and return transfer to your hotel.

■ LIVE MUSIC

Tünel's Asmalı Mescit area in the Beyoğlu neighborhood is popular for its live music, from traditional Turkish to imported Indie and homegrown jazz. **Babylon** *(Şehbender Sokak 3, tel 0212 292 7368, $$$, babylon.com .tr)* has an English-language website that lists nightly shows ranging from dub reggae to Turkish disco. Live sets have included Macy Gray and The Wailers. Opt for **Kloster** *(Kamer Hatun Caddesi 10, tel 0533 258 9393, kloster.com.tr)* for a lineup of international DJs, or walk downhill just past the **Galata Tower** (Galata Kulesi; see pp. 110–111) for live jazz and soul at **Nardis** *(Kuledibi Sokak 14, tel 0212 244 6327, $$$, nardisjazz.com)*. This bare-brick venue attracts a hip, clued-up crowd who love their beats.

■ MEYHANES

A traditional Turkish restaurant is called a *meyhane*—the name derives from the old Anatolian words for wine *(mey)* and house or tavern *(hane)*. These unpretentious establishments

Tünel's lively *meyhanes* spill out onto the streets in summer.

dish up late-night suppers of fish and meze chased down with wine and rakı. For the best *meyhanes*, head to the Asmalı Mescit zone in the Beyoğlu neighborhood or around the **Beşiktaş market** (see p. 147) in the Bosporus & Nişantaşı neighborhood.

In the former, **Yakup 2** (*Asmalı Mescit Caddesi 35, tel 0212 249 2925, $$–$$$*) bustles with family celebrations and the occasional Turkish celebrity. In Beşiktaş, local favorite **Çarşı Balık** (*Köyiçi Caddesi Leşker Sokak 4, tel 0212 258 1841, $$*) serves up marinated tuna, oil-fried mussels, and grilled sea bream. Wherever you go, expect a team of traveling musicians playing traditional Turkish instruments to drop in for a four- or five-song live music set. In both neighborhoods, the dining and drinking go on until late.

■ Wharves & Warehouses

For urban bars, join Istanbul's hipsters in the once-edgy suburb of Karaköy, the city's answer to Brooklyn in New York or Shoreditch in London. Warehouses and wharves have been converted into industrial-chic restaurants and bars. From spring through fall, many spill out onto the narrow, ivy-lined streets that are dotted with strings of twinkling lights. Surprisingly, the hottest new places specialize mostly in house-ground coffee.

For something stronger, try **Colonie** (*Kemankeş Caddesi 87, tel 0212 243 2103, $$$*) for cocktails mixed by outrageously mustachioed locals. Those in the know head to **Ferah Feza** (*Kemankeş Caddesi 31, tel 0212 243 5154, $$$, ferahfeza-ist .com*), which occupies an entire Karaköy rooftop and boasts sublime views across to Galata. To enter, walk through the Istanbul Architectural Institute on ground level, then take the elevator to the fifth floor.

For an after-dinner treat in this neighborhood, try friendly Lebanese patisserie **Pim** (*Kılıç Ali Paşa Mescidi Sokak 12, tel 0212 243 4446, $*), for their rakı-scented truffles.

■ NARGILE CAFÉS

Until a decade or two ago, *nargiles* —otherwise known as sheeshas, hookahs, or water pipes—were an old man's preserve. Their current popularity is such that young guys drinking beer and women sipping cappuccinos puff away all evening throughout the city. The trendiest *nargile* cafés stud both the **Galata Bridge** (see pp. 113–114) itself and the **Tophane** (see pp. 114–115) neighborhood, where there is a line of establishments just behind the **Istanbul Modern** (see pp. 116–117) art gallery. Here, you can recline on beanbags in **Nargilem Café** (*Tophane Salı Pazarı Sıra Mağazalar, tel 0212 244 2492, $$, nargilemcafe.com.tr*).

Alternatively, head to the gloriously atmospheric **Erenler** (*Yeniçeriler Caddesi 35, $$*) in the Southern Golden Horn neighborhood, for more historic surroundings. Turkish lampshades hang from the ceiling and vines cover courtyard walls, as an aromatic smoke scents the air.

■ SUPERCLUBS

A string of self-proclaimed superclubs line the star-studded Kuruçeşme shore in the Bosporus neighborhood. Actors Uma Thuman and Daniel Craig hit these waterside dance floors when in town. The vibrant scene is packed with Turkish footballers, Ukrainian models, soap-opera stars, and gold-diggers of all persuasions—and it's enormous fun. The paparazzi quite literally camp outside until dawn. King of the bling is decade-old **Reina** (*Muallim Naci Caddesi 44, tel 0212 259 5919, $$$$,* *reina.com.tr*). Despite the alleged door policy, if you turn up looking sharp and speaking English you'll most likely be welcomed. They'll roll out the red carpet if you arrive by Ferrari or, as some do, by speedboat. Slightly more sober, but comparatively pricey, is nearby **Sortie** (*Muallim Naci 142, tel 0212 327 8585, $$$$, www.eksenistanbul.com/en/sortie*), where no fewer than seven different restaurants surround a central dance floor. For luxury clubbing without the B-list celebrities, drive five minutes down the coast to **Anjelique** (*Salhane Sokak 5, tel 0212 327 2844, $$$, anjelique.com.tr*). The club's restaurant specializes in seafood carpaccio, while the resident DJ does a fine line in hands-in-the-air Turkish and Euro pop.

NARGILE **SMOKING**

Joining the locals to try a nargile for yourself is easy. First choose a flavor—apple (*elma*) is a good choice for beginners. Your water pipe will arrive with a plastic packaged mouthpiece to ensure hygiene, and a pile of burning embers on top of the tobacco pile. Gently suck to produce a bubble of water-chilled smoke. Take your time with a good book or a game of backgammon—this is a leisurely hour-long pursuit.

Revelers party under a full moon at the Reina superclub overlooking the Bosporus.

Bosporus &
Nişantaşı

For locals, the Bosporus is not simply a strait, but a way of life. Istanbul's seafaring past is glorified in the Maritime Museum, whose windows overlook the strait. From here, former fishing villages such as Ortaköy stretch all the way to the Black Sea. Locals flock to these seaside spots to enjoy the fresh air. The construction of Dolmabahçe Palace by Sultan Abdülmecid I was instrumental in transforming this area of former hunting grounds and villages into an urban center. Borrowing stylistically from European trends of its time, Dolmabahçe Palace is built on the Bosporus, while Yıldız Palace, built later, is set in a wooded park. Inland, on top of a hill, Abdülmecid built Nişantaşı, these days a fashionably eclectic neighborhood and home to some of the city's best shopping.

◐ **The floodlit Büyük
Mecidiye Mosque on the
banks of the Bosporus
in Ortaköy, with the
Bosporus Bridge
in the distance**

Bosporus & Nişantaşı

*Explore architectural delights of the 19th century, then
shop 'til you drop before relaxing with a cocktail.*

BOSPORUS & NIŞANTAŞI

❶ **Dolmabahçe Palace** (see pp. 152-153) Pass through ornate rococo gates to explore the Ottoman Empire's finest 19th-century palace. Walk east on tree-lined Dolmabahçe Caddesi.

❷ **Maritime Museum** (see pp. 146-147) Admire the imperial barges before heading to the basement for a history lesson. Cross the street to enter Süleyman Seba Caddesi.

**NİŞANTAŞI DISTANCE: 6.5 MILES (10.5 KM)
TIME: APPROX. 9 HOURS   TRAM START: KABATAŞ**

Yıldız Palace
(Yıldız Sarayı)
5

Yıldız Park
(Yıldız Parkı)
4

6 **Ortaköy**

Büyük Mecidiye Mosque
(Büyük Mecidiye Camii)

ÇIRAĞAN CAD.

PALANGA CAD.

ÇERVİRMECİ CAD.

DEREBOYU CAD.

YILDIZ

YILDIZ KORUSU

MÜVEZZİ CAD.

D-100

O-1

osporus)

```
0                    400 meters
0                    400 yards
```

7 Nişantaşı (see p. 151)
Peruse the artisan and
designer shops before
winding down with a
cocktail at one of the
neighborhood's many bars.

6 Ortaköy
(see pp. 150-151) Enjoy
the buzz of this popular
seaside resort, then step
into its waterfront mosque.
Hail a cab for Nişantaşı.

4 Yıldız Park (see p. 148) Walk among
the magnolia and Judas trees or have
a refreshment at one of two imperial
pavilions. Exit through the main gates, walk
west to Müvezzi Caddesi, then north.

5 Yıldız Palace
(see pp. 148-149) Imagine
being a sultan yourself, as
you admire the exquisite
Yıldız porcelain on display.
Take a cab to Ortaköy.

3 Beşiktaş (see p. 147) Browse the best of the chic boutiques
before exploring the heart of this colorful district. Make your way
to Barbaros Bulvari and catch a taxi to Yıldız Park.

Dolmabahçe Palace

1 See pp. 152–153.

Dolmabahçe Caddesi • tel 0212 236 9000 • Closed Mon., Thurs., and Jan. 1
• $$$ (includes guided tour in English) • Tram: Kabataş • www.millisaraylar.gov.tr

Maritime Museum

2 Istanbul's Maritime Museum (Deniz Müzesi) underwent extensive restoration in 2013. The architecture alone is impressive—take a moment to appreciate the sheer size of the building and the views of the Bosporus from the floor-to-ceiling windows. En route to the main gallery, you'll pass imposing busts of Ottoman Navy commanders and a number of traditional fishing boats used by Atatürk. The main gallery houses the world's only original intact galley, as well as a collection of wooden ceremonial boats and barges that took sultans, royal ladies, and palace officials

Wooden imperial barges at the Maritime Museum, with richly decorated hulls

to Friday prayers at waterfront mosques. The boats are not roped off, so you can observe all the features in detail—from the elaborate prows and sterns to the ostentatious curtained kiosks. Before climbing to the second floor, which houses more imperial barges, pause at the gilded lion figurehead. For history buffs, weaponry, uniforms, and paintings in the basement gallery paint a detailed picture of the Ottoman Navy's long history.

IN **THE KNOW**

The Maritime Museum has a collection of 13 figureheads. The tradition of decorating ships with figureheads was popular from the 16th to the 19th centuries. The Ottomans favored lions, albatrosses, eagles, falcons, and horses, the majority of which were made in workshops at the Kasımpaşa docks in Istanbul.

Sinanpaşa Mahallesi • tel 0212 327 4345 • Closed Mon. and Jan 1. • $ • Tram: Kabataş; Bus: 28, 28T, 40, or 23B • www.denizmuzeleri.tsk.tr/en

Beşiktaş

③ Hugging the Bosporus shoreline, Beşiktaş is a lively area in which local stores intermingle with trendy coffee houses catering to students and creative types. Start at **Akaretler,** the neighborhood's upmarket quarter, where two rows of town houses (the former residences of Dolmabahçe Palace's high-ranking officials) are now home to boutiques, galleries, and restaurants. On Şair Nedim Caddesi, you'll find exhibits by local artists at **Rampa** (*No. 21a, tel 212 327 0800, closed Mon.*) and **C.A.M. Galeri** (*No. 25, tel 0212 245 7975*). East of here, at the neighborhood market (Mumcu Bakkal Sokak), fishmongers offer their catch of the day, while nearby restaurants sell cheap, tasty fish sandwiches for a quick and filling lunch. In front of the ferry station, **Barbaros Square** (Barbaros Meydanı) takes its name from Admiral Barbaros Hayrettin Paşa, better known as Barbarossa. There's a sculpture of him at the center of the square. His tomb, built by Mimar Sinan in 1542, is here, too. If you're visiting on a Friday, the only day the tomb is open (*1 p.m.–5 p.m.*), peek inside to see the admiral's hat on top of the casket.

Intersection of Şair Nedim Caddessi and Sinan Paşa Köprü Sokak • Tram: Kabataş; Bus: 28 , 28T, 40, or 23B

GOOD **EATS**

■ **KANTIN**
Expect a rotating daily menu of homemade Turkish cuisine with a modern twist at this Nişantaşı favorite. Sample the wafer-thin savory pastries called *çıtır*. Akkavak Sokak 30, tel 0212 219 31 14, $$

■ **KARADENIZ PIDE, DÖNER SALONU**
This hole-in-the-wall kiosk is a neighborhood institution. It is worth waiting in line for tender meat from the spit served in fresh bread with all the trimmings. Mumcu Bakkal Sokak 6, tel 0212 261 7693, $

■ **SIDIKA MEZE**
Feast on excellent Aegean-style seafood in a romantic setting. Highlights include sea bass wrapped in vine leaves. Şair Nedim Caddesi 38, tel 0212 259 7232, $$

Yıldız Park

④ The 600,000-square-yard (500,000 sq m) Yıldız Park (Yıldız Parkı), was part of a forest during Byzantine times and used as a hunting ground during the 15th and 16th centuries. It belonged to the imperial estate from the reign of Sultan Ahmed I (r. 1603–1617) onward.

The highlight here is the **Yıldız Chalet Museum** (Yıldız Şale Köşkü; *closed Mon., Thurs., and Jan. 1, $$, guided tours only*). Abdülhamid II built it in the style of a Swiss chalet for his guest, Kaiser Wilhelm II. Today, the building houses a collection of exquisite rugs and furnishings, including the world's largest Hereke carpet. Hailing from the small coastal town of Hereke, close to Istanbul, these fine carpets are pinnacles of the Turkish weaving tradition, hand-knotted from silk, wool, cotton, and gold thread.

You can reach the chalet on foot, but given the size of the park, it makes sense to take a taxi from the main gates. If exploring the park on foot—much of it is planted with rare and exotic plants and trees—all attractions are clearly signposted. As you go, you may spot two other 19th-century imperial mansions—both former hunting lodges, now restaurants. **Çadır Kiosk** (Çadır Köşkü) looks out onto a lake and has views of the Bosporus, while **Malta Kiosk** (Malta Köşkü) looks into the woodlands.

Yıldız Mahallesi • Bus: 22, 22C, 40, 40A

Yıldız Palace

⑤ The Yıldız Palace (Yıldız Sarayı) is the focus of an impressive complex that represents the heart of the Ottoman Empire in its final years. Set within beautiful grounds, the buildings here include pavilions, factories, mosques, museums, and a theater. Work started here during the first half of the 19th century, but it was Abdülhamid II who commissioned most of the structures you see today, in the 1870s. The Italian architect Raimondo D'Aronco aided the principal architect, Sarkis Balyan, in designing some of the pavilions, including the **Armory** with its majestic Corinthian columns (just opposite the palace as you approach).

Focus your visit on the ground floor of the palace, which is now a museum. After purchasing a ticket, stroll through the gallery displaying artworks, gifts, and furniture from the imperial household, among them several porcelain masterpieces from the former **Yıldız Porcelain Factory** (tel 0212 260 2370, closed Sat., Sun., and Jan. 1, $), located within **Yıldız Park.** The adjacent gallery houses Abdülhamid II's carpentry workshop, complete with his tools. Continue to the state apartments, and a hamam decorated with delightful turquoise and white tiles. Allow some time to explore the grounds of the palace, with their ornate fountains, wooden kiosks, and far fewer people than you'll encounter at **Topkapı Palace** (Topkapı Sarayı; see pp. 62–65) or **Dolmabahçe Palace** (Dolmabahçe Sarayı; see pp. 152–153). Before leaving, stop to admire one of the only pavilions dating back to the reign of Abdülaziz (r. 1861–1876)—the lavish **State Apartments** (Büyük Mabeyn), currently a restaurant.

Serencebey Yokuşu 62 • Tel 0212 258 3080 • Closed Tues. • $ • Bus: 28, 28T, 40 and 23B • yildizsarayi.com.tr

One of several marble fountains on the grounds of Yıldız Palace

Ortaköy

6 The waterside district of Ortaköy has, at its heart, **İskele Meydanı,** a buzzing seaside square surrounded by a labyrinth of souvenir stores. Behind the square on Mecidiye Köprüsü Sokak is a row of baked potato *(kumpir)* stands ready to pile your potato with any ingredient imaginable. The square draws a crowd on weekends, when an all-day market sets up, selling artworks, crafts, handmade clothing, secondhand books, and jewelry.

If visiting during the week, you'll find more boutiques and galleries on Muallim Naci Caddesi, to the east along the seafront. Don't miss **Simya Galeri** *(No. 51, tel 0212 259 7740)*, which displays artist Sabrina Fresko's small-scale sculptures and unique jewelry. Beneath the west corner of the Bosporus Bridge—right on the waterfront—you'll find the neoclassical **Büyük Mecidiye Mosque** (Büyük Mecidiye Camii). The interior has a different mood to most

A glassblower demonstrates his skills at creating a whirling dervish, Ortaköy street market.

other mosques: Lighter and brighter, all pinks and creams and brass chandeliers, the place feels more like a ballroom than a mosque. To the east of the mosque, boats vie to take visitors up and down the Bosporus. **Plan Tours** *(tel 0212 234 7777, $$$$, plantours.com)* and **Bosphorus Tours** *(tel 0554 797 2646, $$$$, bosphorustour.com)* offer full-day and half-day cruises with guides and food included. Check websites for pickup points.

Vapur İskelesi Sokak • Bus: 22, 22C, 40, and 40A

Nişantaşı

If you have come to Istanbul to shop, Nişantaşı is the place to do it. You'll find everything here from designer dresses to traditional rugs and even works of art. Start your tour at the neo-baroque **Teşvikiye Mosque** (Teşvikiye Camii; *Teşvikiye Caddesi*) and cut through to the narrow, boutique-filled **Atiye Sokak,** where **Nord & Sud** *(No. 12)* stocks household objects in Nordic and Provençal styles. Head to perpendicular **Abdi İpekçi Caddesi** where local luxury designers cohabit with high-fashion brands such as Gucci, Prada, and Louis Vuitton. **Machka** *(No. 44)* stocks sophisticated dresses by award-winning fashion duo Dice Kayek, while **Armaggan** *(No. 8)* sells precious gemstone jewelry. On parallel **Mim Kemal Öke Caddesi**, the auction house **Portakal** *(No. 8)* sells art by Ottoman and contemporary artists including Diaz De La Peña and Marc Quinn. End your day with a cocktail at **Den** *(No. 1D, tel 0212 224 2470)*. Other good bars are the lively **Biber Bar** *(Abdi İpekçi Caddesi 36, tel 0212 231 4106)* or **Frankie** *(Teşvikiye Caddesi 41A, tel 0212 230 6666)* on the rooftop of the Sofa Hotel, with live music *(Tues.–Thurs.)*.

Intersection of Teşvikiye Caddesi and Atiye Sokak • Metro: Osmanbey

IN **THE KNOW**

Not far from the shopping district of Nişantaşı is the **Atatürk Museum** (Atatürk Müzesi; *Halaskargazi Caddesi 250, tel 0212 233 4723, closed Mon. and Sun.*). The former Turkish president once lived here, and the three-story house now displays a number of his personal belongings, including medals, military uniforms, and photographs.

Dolmabahçe Palace

*Experience the style and luxury in which the Ottoman
sultans lived at this sumptuous palace.*

The crystal banisters of this impressive staircase were made by the French glassworks Baccarat.

In the 19th century, Sultan Abdülmecid I abandoned the traditional Topkapı
Palace residence and commissioned the Dolmabahçe Palace (Dolmabahçe
Sarayı). The brief was for something modern. Much of the interior design was
the work of Charles Séchan (known for the Paris Opéra). The result combines
elements of baroque, rococo, and neoclassical style alongside traditional
Islamic design. A grand ceremonial hall *(Muayede)* is flanked on either side
by the business quarters *(Selamlık)* and the family quarters *(Harem)*.

■ Business Matters

The *Selamlık* tour (see sidebar this page) starts in the **Secretarial Chambers.** Admire the 79-foot-long (24 m) painting, **"The Sürre Procession"** of a pilgrimage to Mecca, before making your way to a crystal staircase (the guide will position you to get the best view before you make the climb).

Upstairs, a tour of the **Royal Floor** reveals rooms with exquisite fireplaces and porcelain stoves as well as the sultan's Egyptian alabaster marble hamam. Step into the **Red Hall,** where sultans received family members, and your eyes are immediately drawn to the ceiling, where Séchan's signature French flair is evident. The tour finishes at the *Muayede,* with the world's largest Bohemian crystal chandelier, a gift from Great Britain's Queen Victoria in the late 1800s.

■ Living Quarters

Highlights of the Harem tour are on the first floor. Start in the **Blue Hall,** originally reserved for ceremonies and religious holidays, which takes its name from the draperies and upholstery on show. Look up to see another of

SAVVY **TRAVELER**

The palace admits just 3,000 visitors per day and you must join a guided tour (given in English). The ticket office opens at 9 a.m. and closes when the quota has been met, so arrive early to be sure to get in. A standard ticket includes a 45-minute tour of the *Muayede* and *Selamlık*. Other options include a tour of just the *Harem,* or a full ticket, which covers the *Muayede, Selamlık, Harem,* and the palace grounds.

Séchan's remarkable ceilings, the corners of which feature gold-leaf panels decorated with landscapes of the four seasons. Peek into opulent guest rooms peppered with Japanese and Chinese artworks. Finally, visit Atatürk's carefully preserved bedroom. The Turkish president died in this room, and the clock is set at 9:05 a.m. —the exact time of his death.

■ The Imperial Grounds

Pretty fountains, sculptures, and pavilions are scattered throughout the grounds. Visit the **Crystal Pavilion**—a glass conservatory with a striking water feature and statues of peacocks in a kaleidoscope of colors.

BOSPORUS & NİŞANTAŞI

Dolmabahçe Caddesi • tel 0212 236 9000 • Closed Mon., Thurs., and Jan. 1 • $$$ (includes guided tour in English) • Tram: Kabataş • www.millisaraylar.gov.tr

Turkish Textiles

The Turkish are obsessed with textiles. From the Ottoman era to modern times, textiles have held an important place in the city, both culturally and as goods to be traded both in Turkey and around the world. Patterned fabrics fashioned into scarves, kaftans, cushion covers, blankets, and bold-colored carpets adorn shop windows from the Old City to Nişantaşı—and few visitors can resist taking something home with them.

A 17th-century Turkish textile made from silk and metal thread, embroidered with tulips
Opposite: Carpet sellers display their wares outside the Grand Bazaar.

History & Techniques

Although the country produces around 650 different fabrics, the Turks are especially good at weaving silk. In Ottoman times, ambassadors to Europe showered heads of state with gifts of luxurious silk brocade (*çatma*)—upholstery, cushion covers, and kaftans. At the time, workshops in Üsküdar became famous for decorating such gifts in a style that has become known as "Turkish rococo."

Turkish carpets and rugs were traditionally either hand-knotted or flat-woven and came in a variety of styles, with *kilim* (a flat tapestry-woven carpet used for decoration or praying) and *cicim* (handmade wool rugs comprising colored strips) among the most common. Even today, carpet makers follow the same traditional techniques. Another uniquely Turkish technique, known as "a thousand pieces," was used by imperial tailors at the **Topkapı Palace** (Topkapı Sarayı; see pp. 62–65) to make fine patchwork fabrics.

True to their extravagant nature, these craftsmen used dizzying motifs of flowers, trees, animals, birds, crescent moons, stars, and fruit.

Modern Times

Traditional textile techniques live on today. Carpet traders commission designs by artists, which are then hand-loomed. For some of the best, visit Mehmet Güreli's **Dhoku** and **EthniCon** stores, both in the Grand Bazaar. **Mehmet Çetinkaya** (*Küçük Ayasofya Caddesi, Tavukhane Sokak 7*) in Sultanahmet has a collection of robes in a variety of patterns that look just as they would have done in the early 19th century, when the technique first came into vogue. Fashion brand **Dice Kayek** makes handwoven dresses in lamé brocade, not unlike robes worn by Ottoman rulers.

TEXTILE **SHOPS**

Gönül Paksoy This best-loved Turkish designer transforms traditional fabrics into interesting wearable garments that evoke modern Sufi dervish robes. **Atiye Sokak 1/3–4, tel 0212 236 0209**

Güneş Öztarakçı This was the first rug store opened in Istanbul by a woman. You'll find antique rugs, Anatolian kilims, and vegetable-dyed carpets. **Mim Kemal Öke Caddesi 5, tel 0212 225 1954**

Yastık Against stark white walls, Rıfat Özbek's colorful cushions sewn from antique *ikat* fabrics stand out from the crowd. **Şakayık Sokak 13/1, tel 0212 240 8731**

City Views

Hilly topography and a minaret-pierced skyline make Istanbul the perfect place for stunning city views. The Golden Horn and Bosporus sparkle by day while city lights twinkle by night. Join Istanbullus at one of the city's many vantage points—from ancient ramparts and hilltop cafés to hip rooftop bars.

BOSPORUS & NISANTASI

■ RUMELI FORTRESS

The 15th-century Rumeli Fortress (Rumelihisarı) lies on the western bank of the Bosporus just north of Nişantaşı. Mehmet the Conqueror strategically chose the narrowest point of the strait as his location in order to have control of the traffic. Climb any one of the three main towers for sweeping views of the strait and the **Fatih Sultan Mehmet Bridge.** If you are afraid of heights or are traveling with small children, bear in mind that there are no railings here.

Yahya Kemal Caddesi 42 • Closed Wed.
• $ • Bus: 40

■ GÜLHANE PARK CAFÉ

Not only an ideal place to rest your feet while exploring the Old City, **Gülhane Park** (Gülhane Parkı; see pp. 57–58) also has a hilltop café from which to enjoy impressive views of ships moving across the Bosporus while sipping tea poured from a traditional teapot (*semaver).* There are scores of tables and chairs on the terraces here, and a kiosk that serves giant baked potatoes.

Alemdar Caddesi • Tram: Gülhane

■ PIERRE LOTI CAFÉ

For unparalleled views of the Golden Horn, don't miss this pretty outdoor café on top of a hill in the Eyüp neighborhood (see p. 97). Both hill and café are named after the French novelist and self-professed Turkophile, Pierre Loti, who is said to have sought inspiration for his novels here. Order Turkish pancakes (*gözleme*) with your drink, lean back, and watch the world go by. The café is crowded on weekends, when tables closest to the edge become a prized commodity.

İdris Köşkü Caddesi • tel: 0212 497 1313 • $
• Bus 55 • pierrelotitepesi.com

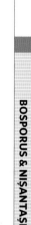

![The viewing platform on Pierre Loti Hill, with the Golden Horn stretching into the distance]

The viewing platform on Pierre Loti Hill, with the Golden Horn stretching into the distance

■ 360 ISTANBUL

For dinner with a view, few venues rival this slick restaurant in Beyoğlu. On the eighth floor above **İstiklal Caddesi** (see pp. 134–135), this bar and restaurant has, as its name suggests, a circular terrace offering stunning, 360-degree views over the city. Equally charming for a sunny terrace lunch or nightime dining amid twinkling city lights, this is the perfect choice for a splash-out meal. They have an excellent selection of Turkish wines.

İstiklal Caddesi 163 • tel 0212 251 1042 • $$$–$$$$ • Metro: Taksim • 360istanbul.com

■ ÇAMLICA HILL

Çamlıca Hill in Asian Istanbul is the city's highest point, rising 880 feet (268 m) above sea level. Vistas stretch across the city and all the way to the Princes Islands (see pp. 172–173). From this vantage point, you can really appreciate Istanbul's size. There are a number of cafés on the grounds as well as a popular picnic area. This also happens to be a primary stopover for migrating birds in the spring, so don't forget to bring your binoculars if bird-watching is your thing.

Çamlıca Tepesi • Bus 6t

Marmara Denizi
(Sea of Marmara)

Asian Istanbul

In many respects, Asian Istanbul is richer, more historic, and more glamorous than its European cousin. Furthermore, despite being a short boat ride from Sultanahmet, this collection of Bosporus villages—now one long suburban sprawl separated by parks and cemeteries—is almost entirely tourist-free. You'll see only locals at Üsküdar's main attractions: its three spellbinding mosques—Mihrimah Sultan, Atik Valide, and Şakirin—

ASIAN ISTANBUL

each markedly different to the others in style and atmosphere. The entire area offers a taste of true Turkey, with fruit-juice vendors, antique dealers, and local traders at every turn. Conversely, for fish, wine, and upscale eats, it doesn't get any better than quaint Kuzguncuk, buzzy Kadıköy, or classy Moda. All three are hotspots for actors, aristocrats, and Turkey's cultural elite. Tea gardens and kebab stops are plentiful, and offer welcome respite from sauntering, sightseeing, and shopping.

◀ **Locals lunch on a
cobbled sidewalk
at just one of many
restaurants and
cafés in the one-time
village of Kuzguncuk.**

Asian Istanbul

Minarets, parks, shops, and markets make conservative Üsküdar and liberal Kadıköy two of the most vibrant neighborhoods in Istanbul.

❶ Beylerbeyi Palace (see p. 162) Explore the rococo halls of the palace. From just outside the gates, take any bus cruising south. Alight at Üryanizade Sokak in Kuzguncuk.

❷ Kuzguncuk Village (see p. 163) Admire the charming, brightly painted cafés in this erstwhile Bosporus village. Hop aboard any southbound bus to Üsküdar.

0 — 200 meters
0 — 200 yards

❸ Mihrimah Sultan Mosque (see p. 163) After exploring the imposing building, leave by the side exit to reach Selmani Pak Caddesi. Meander uphill—walking west on Kara Gazi Caddesi, then south on Evliya Hoca Sokak and Çavuşdere Caddesi.

❹ Atik Valide Mosque (see pp. 168-169) Drink a glass of tea in the shaded gardens. Walk south on Kartal Baba Caddesi, then west on Nuhkuyusu Caddesi to Karacaahmet Cemetery.

Maiden's Tower (Kız Kulesi) ❻

Mihrimah Sultan Mosque (Mihrimah Sultan Camii) ❸

Üsküdar

DOĞANCILAR CAD.

HALK CAD.

HAREM

SAHİL YOLU CAD.

GÜNDOĞUMU

TUNUSBAĞI C.

TIBBİYE C.

❺ Şakirin Mosque (see pp. 164-165) The mosque sits on the northern flank of the cemetery. Walk northwest on Tunusbağı Caddesi and then Salacak İskele Caddesi to find the ferry in Salacak.

❻ Maiden's Tower (see p. 165) Refuel in the panoramic café. Back on shore, take a taxi east on Söğütlüçeşme Caddesi and south on Güneşlibahçe Sokak to Kadıköy.

ASIAN ISTANBUL DISTANCE: 13.5 MILES (22 KM)
TIME: APPROX. 9 HOURS START: BEYLERBEYI PALACE

ASIAN ISTANBUL

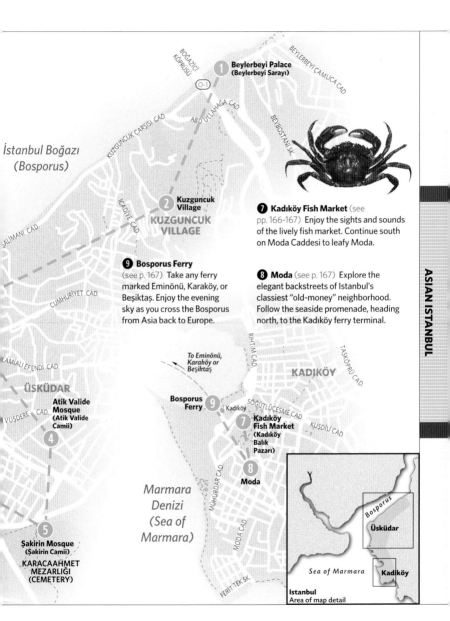

Beylerbeyi Palace
(Beylerbeyi Sarayı)

İstanbul Boğazı
(Bosporus)

② **Kuzguncuk Village**

KUZGUNCUK VILLAGE

⑦ **Kadıköy Fish Market** (see pp. 166-167) Enjoy the sights and sounds of the lively fish market. Continue south on Moda Caddesi to leafy Moda.

⑨ **Bosporus Ferry** (see p. 167) Take any ferry marked Eminönü, Karaköy, or Beşiktaş. Enjoy the evening sky as you cross the Bosporus from Asia back to Europe.

⑧ **Moda** (see p. 167) Explore the elegant backstreets of Istanbul's classiest "old-money" neighborhood. Follow the seaside promenade, heading north, to the Kadıköy ferry terminal.

ASIAN ISTANBUL

To Eminönü, Karaköy or Beşiktaş

KADIKÖY

Bosporus Ferry **⑨** Kadıköy

ÜSKÜDAR

Atik Valide Mosque
(Atik Valide Camii)

④

⑦ **Kadıköy Fish Market**
(Kadıköy Balık Pazarı)

Marmara Denizi
(Sea of Marmara)

⑧ **Moda**

⑤

Şakirin Mosque
(Şakirin Camii)

KARACAAHMET MEZARLIĞI (CEMETERY)

Bosporus

Üsküdar

Sea of Marmara   **Kadıköy**

Istanbul
Area of map detail

Guests at the Beylerbeyi Palace often arrived by boat, disembarking on the rococo landing platform.

Beylerbeyi Palace

During the second half of the 19th century, a new generation of Turkish leaders built European-style palaces on the banks of the Bosporus. Among them, the 30-room Beylerbeyi Palace (Beylerbeyi Sarayı) is an East-meets-West mini-Versailles. Its name translates as Lord of Lords, and it is the work of Sarkis Balyan, whose father built the **Dolmabahçe Palace** (Dolmabahçe Sarayı; see pp. 152–153) across the water. The design pairs Roman columns with Ottoman swirls. Linger a while in the sultan's bedroom, and you can visualize its one-time occupant smoking a water pipe between mouthfuls of Turkish delight served on French Sèvres porcelain. In the palace gardens along the waterfront, are a women-only bathing kiosk and the ornate stone landing platform.

Abdullahağa Caddesi • tel 0216 321 9320 • Closed Mon., Thurs. • $$ • Bus: 15 • www.millisaraylar.gov.tr

Kuzguncuk Village

2 Overlooking the Bosporus, the former village of Kuzguncuk has a low-key vibe that has attracted Istanbul's elite for centuries. Lose yourself in its maze of streets with their sidewalk cafés and seek out the pastel houses that line **Üryanizade Sokak.** A number of the country's highest rollers—including many Turkish actors—live in the wooden waterside mansions *(yalı)* visible along **Kuzguncuk Çarşısı Caddesi,** the road that follows the seafront. You can see the finest of these, **Ahmet Fethi Paşa Yalısı,** the former home of the Ottoman ambassador to Paris, at its southern end. Although closed to the public, you can't miss the building as you pass by on the bus—the white clapboard mansion literally leans over the Bosporus. Other village highlights include a number of leafy Greek and Jewish cemeteries of yesteryear, most notably those on **İcadiye Caddesi,** one of the village's main thoroughfares.

Intersection of Kuzguncuk Çarşısı Caddesi and İcadiye Caddesi • Bus: 15

Mihrimah Sultan Mosque

3 The great Ottoman architect Mimar Sinan (see p. 68) designed the Mihrimah Sultan Mosque (Mihrimah Sultan Camii) in 1548, for Sultan Süleyman the Magnificent's favorite daughter. On entering, sit beneath the brooding dome within, just behind where the congregation normally sit. The highlight here is the finely frescoed ceiling that soars skyward in a kaleidoscope of red, green, and blue. Watch the light stream through stained-glass windows onto the recently restored granite columns and marble surrounds. Even the antique door handles shimmer, just as they would have during the 16th century.

Hakimiyeti Milliye Caddesi • Closed Fri. and during prayer times • Metro: Üsküdar

IN **THE KNOW**

Mimar Sinan designed a second mosque in honor of Mihrimah, near **Chora Church** (Kariye Müzesi; see pp. 98–99) in Edirnekapı. Both were built according to precise calculations. On March 21—by coincidence both Mihrimah's birthday and the spring equinox—as the fiery sun sets behind the Edirnekapı minaret, the moon simultaneously rises between the twin minarets of the mosque in Üsküdar.

Atik Valide Mosque

See pp. 168–169.

Valide-i Atik Mahallesi • Closed Fri. and during prayer times • Metro: Üsküdar

Şakirin Mosque

Among Istanbul's most accessible—and most wonderful—mosques, the Şakirin Mosque (Şakirin Camii) was built in 2009. Its female architect, Zeynep Fadıllıoğlu, was the first woman to design a mosque in Turkey, and the result is a bold statement of sexual equality in one of Istanbul's most traditional quarters. Walk through the main doors, and you'll see immediately how Ottoman showiness has been channeled into modern mosque style.

Straight ahead, the sky-blue prayer area, with its beaten copper interior, would not seem out of place in a boutique hotel. Above, glass-bead chandeliers embedded with tiny teardrops drip down

A sculptural fountain is the focus of the tranquil courtyard at the Şakirin Mosque.

from the ceiling in concentric circles. Three interwoven rings that surround the chandeliers are engraved with Arabic script listing Islam's 99 names of God—Allah, Ar-Rahman, Ar-Rahim, Al-Malik …Uniquely, the women's prayer area in this mosque is just as sublime as that for men, and female visitors have a clear view of the magnificent chandelier. Just beyond the mosque's glass walls lies the immense and hugely atmospheric **Karacaahmet Cemetery**—with origins dating back as far as the 14th century.

Nuhkuyusu Caddesi 2 • Closed Fri. and during prayer times • Bus: 3, 13 • sakirincamii.net

Maiden's Tower

6 As well as providing the backdrop for scenes in two James Bond movies and spawning a dozen legends—the Maiden's Tower (Kız Kulesi) has also featured on a Turkish banknote. Lying just 490 feet (150 m) off the Üsküdar shoreline, it is one of Istanbul's landmarks. The romance starts along the pedestrian-only Üsküdar boardwalk, as you pass fishermen casting their lines in front of the Şemsi Paşa Mosque. Ride one of the ferries that chug across from the tiny harbor of Salacak (*daily, 9 a.m. to 6:45 p.m.*) to the tower. Step ashore on the island and wander around the tower. It functioned as a customs station in Roman times. Then, a millennium ago, it became a watchtower and, during the 16th century, a lighthouse. It has also served as a quarantine post, a semaphore station, and a home for retired seamen. Today, the tower houses a panoramic café. Climb to the top floor for tea in the café, where you can snap a selfie from the balcony.

Kız Kulesi • tel 0216 342 4747 • $$ • Bus: 12

GOOD **EATS**

■ **KADI NIMET**
Sit down to the world's freshest seafood at Kadıköy's busiest outlet. Fish stew and squid-stuffed vine leaves feature on the menu. **Tarihi Balıkçılar Çarşısı, Kadıköy 10/A, tel 0216 348 7389, $$**

■ **KANAAT LOKANTASI**
Kanaat, in Üsküdar, has been serving up platters of Anatolian delicacies since 1933. Popular dishes include homemade Circassian chicken and eggplant kebabs. **Selmani Pak Caddesi 9, tel 0216 341 5444, $$**

■ **KOSINITZA**
This inexpensive Franco-Turkish restaurant in elegant Kuzguncuk dishes up squid skewers, shrimp croquettes, and fried anchovies. **L. Bereketli Sokak 2, tel 0216 334 0400, $$**

ASIAN ISTANBUL

Kadıköy Fish Market

7 Two to three blocks south of Kadıköy's port, a bustling daily Fish Market (Kadıköy Balık Pazarı) occupies a crisscross of streets piled high with fish, squid, nuts, and spices. Housewives shop for Anatolian cheese and air-dried pastırma beef, and entire families lunch out on the fried mussel skewers that are sold on almost every pedestrian-only street corner. If you have a sweet tooth, head to **Hacı Bekir** *(Muvakkithane 6/A, tel 0216 336 1519),* which sells handmade sweets (nougat and Turkish delight) made with pressed fruit juice. Then stroll along the most atmospheric street of them all, **Güneşlibahçe Sokak.** This foodie's fantasy of lobster, octopus, Aegean herbs, and Antalya citrus is also home to the **Çiya restaurant empire** (see p. 25). The owner, Musa Dağdeviren, is renowned for his adherence to seasonal cuisine and ancient Anatolian recipes, such as lamb-stuffed beet greens. He

Locals travel from all over the city to buy the enticing produce at Kadıköy Fish Market.

operates three branches of Çiya here—two budget kebab specialists and a gourmet bistro (*sofrası*).

Güneşlibahçe Sokak • Tram: Kadıköy; Bus: 12

Moda

8 Moda is a liberal enclave located a short stroll south of **Kadıköy Fish Market.** Lose yourself amid its leafy warren of streets lined with patisseries, bookstores, and florists. Join Moda locals for an early evening Efes beer (a Turkish brew) along **Moda Caddesi** or drop into **Ali Usta** (*Moda Caddesi 176, tel 0216 414 1880*), one of the district's oldest ice-cream parlors, a neighborhood favorite that wouldn't look out of place on Sunset Boulevard. What attracts most Istanbullus are the seafront café-bars. Best of the bunch is **Koço** (*Moda Caddesi 265*), a 1930s institution that pairs exemplary seafood with fine Turkish wine.

Intersection of Moda Caddesi & Ferit Tek Sokak • Bus: 14-E

Bosporus Ferry

9 The 15-minute ferry hop operated by **Şehir Hatları** ferries (*$, sehirhatlari.com.tr*) from Kadıköy to Eminönü and Karaköy is both a grand voyage and an Istanbul must-see. At dawn and dusk, a large proportion of Istanbul's 14 million residents commute on the many passenger boats that make this journey. Join the evening crowd and order a glass of steaming *çay* from the onboard tea boy as you zip between continents with the wind in your hair (there's room inside to sit on chilly days). Relax and enjoy the scene as Asia, the **Princes Islands** (see pp. 172–173), and the **Maiden's Tower** (Kız Kulesi; see p. 165) drift into the sunset. Tickets are available at any ferry terminal booth and you rarely have to wait in line.

Rıhtım Caddesi • Metro: Kadıköy; Bus: 12

Visitors who have already enjoyed the **Nostalgic Tram** on İstiklal Caddesi (see p. 41) will be thrilled to discover that Moda has a Nostalgic Tram, too. Following a circular route from Moda to Kadıköy, the trams are invariably less busy than their Beyoğlu counterparts.

ASIAN ISTANBUL

Atik Valide Mosque

Mimar Sinan's crowning glory is an Ottoman masterpiece in granite, marble, and vibrant İznik tiles.

The domed interior of the Atik Valide Mosque is a blaze of light and color.

Built in 1583, the Atik Valide Mosque (Atik Valide Camii) is the last major work of Mimar Sinan, the greatest Turkish architect of them all; some say he saved the best until last. Perched on a hill above the suburb of Üsküdar, the mosque dominates the skyline, with twin minarets rising above its large central dome. More than any other religious site in the city, this complex has a relaxed spirit that encourages calm contemplation. Enter the grounds through the imposing stone arch on Tekkeönü Sokak.

■ LEAFY COURTYARD

Follow the domed, stone porticoes that surround the mosque's courtyard gardens in a counterclockwise manner. Mediterranean plane trees rise up from the gardens on your left. Ottoman-era headstones inscribed with Arabic script lean casually against the walls on your right. Soak up the atmosphere in the teahouse midway along the porticoes. Relax as the marble fountain *(şadırvan)* bubbles in the center of the grounds, and the resident cats dart around your feet.

■ OTTOMAN GLORY

Passing through the mosque's handsome double porch entrance, you'll notice that the silent interior is much darker than other mosques. The effect is to concentrate the eye on the Arabesque swirls above, as you soak up the atmospheric ambiance. Look up to see the enormous, central dome resting upon five smaller domes, all beautifully decorated in intricate designs of blue, red, and gold. Antique lights of all shapes and sizes—restored or replaced over the past century—are suspended over the space beneath, in which you'll find both the *mihrab* (altar) and the *minbar* (prayer pulpit).

IN **THE KNOW**

The mosque was built for Nurbanu Sultan, the wife of the generally incapable (and allegedly alcoholic) leader, Sultan Selim II. Venetian-born Nurbanu was the real power behind the Ottoman throne, and the first of several women to have such influence over their sultan husbands during an era referred to as the Rule of the Women. Nurbanu also became *valide* (sultan's mother—a key position in the court) when her son Murad III ascended the throne. It was Murad III who commissioned Sinan to build the mosque in his mother's honor after she died.

■ FINE DETAILS

Exquisite touches remind visitors to the building that this is no ordinary mosque, but one that was designed for the *valide,* the all-powerful mother of the ruling sultan (see sidebar this page). The colorful tiles on either side of the **mihrab** were handmade by the famed artisans of İznik (see p. 79). Close examination of the tiles will reveal popular patterns of the day featuring tulips, birds, blossoms, cypress trees, and leaping fish. The mosque's huge **wooden doors** are inlaid with exquisite mother-of-pearl, while the **minbar** is made from finely carved marble.

Valide-i Atik Mahallesi · Closed Fri. and during prayer times · Metro: Üsküdar

ASIAN ISTANBUL

Hamams

The Turkish steam bath epitomized the mysterious East for centuries. Combining central Asian bathing traditions with those of the Romans in Constantinople, the hamams in Istanbul were often built as gifts to the people from Turkish sultans, pashas, and grand viziers—alongside mosques and fountains. All of them are spectacular, and a simple steam in one of these ancient bathhouses is like attending a class in architecture.

ASIAN ISTANBUL

A classic Turkish massage and wash at the Cağaloğlu Hamam in Sultanahmet
Opposite: Visitors at the Çemberlitaş Hamam look up to a dizzying domed ceiling shot with beams of natural light.

Steamy Backstory

Istanbul's hamams haven't existed for 500 years simply to clean the city's residents. The hamam's popularity continues as a place in which to gossip, doze, and relax away from home life or work pressures. Right up until the 1970s, family matriarchs would interview potential brides for their sons in the bathhouse—assessing their physical attributes, among others. These days, Istanbul's new breed of baths, like the Kılıç Ali Paşa Hamamı in **Tophane** (see pp. 114–115) combine the traditional hamam ritual with an opportunity to purchase hamam luxuries from its boutique.

How to Hamam

Bring a bikini or shorts if you want to, otherwise change into the thin hamam towel (*peştemal*) and sandals provided. Then follow the hamam attendant into the marble-clad steam room. If you've ordered a soap scrub and massage package, a masseur will take you to a quiet corner for an uncompromisingly tough rub. Following a short bath in a less steamy room, you'll be escorted into a cool reclining salon with refreshments. Stay as long as you wish. Payment may be requested on arrival or upon exit depending on the hamam. Add an appropriate tip for the masseur if warranted.

Architectural Gems

The Ottoman Empire's most famous architect, Sinan (see p. 68), was behind the most spectacular city spas. The Çemberlitaş has an intricate *göbek taşı* (hot marble slab) where guests lie supine on entry. His recently reopened **Ayasofya Hamamı** *(Ayasofya Meydanı 2, tel 0212 517 3535, ayasofyahamami.com),* built for Süleyman's wife, Roxelana, offers a near endless vista of marble chambers and wooden recliners.

ISTANBUL **HAMAMS**

Çemberlitaş Hamam
An architectural gem of unsurpassed splendor, occasionally service can be brusque. **Vezirhan Caddesi 8, tel 0212 522 7974, cemberlitashamami.com**

Cinili Hamam Inexpensive neighborhood hamam near the Atik Valide Mosque (see pp. 168–169). **Çavuşdere Caddesi 204, tel 0216 334 9710, cinilihamam.com**

Kılıç Ali Paşa Hamamı
A glittering example of a historic hamam, complete with sumptuous service. **Hamam Sokak 1, tel 0212 393 8010, kilicalipasahamami.com**

ASIAN ISTANBUL

Seaside Escapes

Istanbullus escape the high summer heat by packing picnics, games, and their entire families and heading to the city's shores. For history and elegance in equal measure, the idyllic Princes Islands in the Sea of Marmara are second-to-none, while the Black Sea beaches attract younger and hipper crowds.

■ KINALIADA

Kınalıada is one of the nine forested Princes Islands (Adaları) that lie to the south of Istanbul's Asian coastline. These islands have been a place of high-class retreat for the last millennium, and Kınalıada is the most accessible. A hike around the island takes approximately 90 minutes. You can reach it by ferry (*Şehir Hatları, $, sehirhatlari.com .tr*) from Kadıköy in Asian Istanbul and Kabataş in Europe, with regular departures throughout the day.

■ HEYBELIADA

The ferry that sails to Kınalıada continues on to the second largest Princes Island, Heybeliada, with its long, narrow beaches, 19th-century villas, and a waterfront promenade. To explore on foot, set off from the central square near the ferry terminal and hike around the island's 4.5-mile-long (7 km) coast.

There are plenty of places—some easier to access than others—from which to take a dip in the sea.

■ BÜYÜKADA

Büyükada literally translates as "big island," and it is the largest and most remote of the Princes Islands. Key sights are the seaside boulevard and its main square, both directly in front of the ferry terminal. Tour the island by horse-drawn carriage (*$$$$, adalar .bel.tr*). You'll see them lined up like taxis at the main square. Take a short (*küçük tur*) or long tour (*büyük tur*) along winding leafy lanes, past wooden townhouses and seafront hotels. The high point, quite literally, is a hike, bike, or carriage ride up to the **Aya Yorgi Monastery** at 660 feet (200 m), with the final section accessible only by foot. The adjoining hilltop restaurant offers panoramic views as well as beer and kebabs. Use Şehir Hatları ferries to

Kınalıada's Ayazma Beach draws the biggest crowds in summer.

reach the island or opt for the swifter catarmaran Sea Bus service run by İdo *(tel 0850 222 4436, $$, ido.com.tr)*.

■ KILYOS

Happy crowds frolic on the golden sands of this Black Sea resort, 22 miles (35 km) north of **Galata Bridge** (Galata Köprüsü; see pp. 113–114). Although blissfully quiet much of the year, July and August bring hip beach bars onto the shore. Kitesurfing, windsurfing, and even bodysurfing in the crashing waves are among the most popular activities. To reach the resort, take a Şehir Hatları ferry (see p. 172)

to Sarıyer, from where you can catch a bus *(no. 151)* heading north.

■ ŞILE

Şile is a sleepy fishing village around an hour north of Istanbul and reached by bus from Üsküdar *(Nos. 139 and 139A)*. Laid-back fish restaurants and a looping strip of sand make it an idyllic introduction to Turkish coastal life. Black Sea breezes keep Şile enviably cool as Istanbul swelters in high summer. As with all Black Sea beaches, stiff undercurrents mean that swimming is advisable only under the watchful eye of a lifeguard.

PART 3

Travel Essentials

TRAVEL **ESSENTIALS**

PLANNING YOUR TRIP

When to Go
Istanbul is a city of extremes. Summers can be hot and crowded, while biting winds and snowy skies are hallmarks of winter. The ideal times to visit Istanbul are spring (April, May, June) and fall (September, October, November). During these temperate months, cafés and restaurants spill out onto the city streets, Istanbullus haven't yet decamped to their holiday homes, and there's a general buzzy feel to the city. However, if you do visit in winter or summer, you'll still find a cozy café with an open fire, or a lively bar with a rooftop panorama, to suit your needs.

Istanbul doesn't shut down for major public holidays. But bear in mind that opening hours may shorten. Key dates include **Labour Day** *(May 1),* **Republic Day** *(Oct. 29),* and the anniversary of **Atatürk's death** *(Nov. 9).* During the Islamic holiday of **Ramadan** (which will occur during May and June until 2020) offices and stores, but only a handful of Istanbul sights and restaurants, shut up shop. The same closures occur during the shorter religious celebrations of **Şeker Bayramı** (the three-day holiday that follows Ramadan) and **Kurban Bayramı** (which follows two months and ten days after Şeker Bayramı).

Health Insurance
All visitors to Turkey should be covered by a private heath insurance policy. You may well have to pay for Turkish treatment upfront; be sure to keep evidence of your medical expenses in order to be reimbursed back home. Note that insurance companies will require a police report for any lost or stolen items.

Passports
Most visitors are required to purchase an **e-Visa** before arriving in Turkey. Be sure to check the details of this with your consulate (see p. 179) before traveling.

TO AND FROM THE AIRPORT

Airport
International flights land at one of the city's two airports. Major flag carriers normally use the larger **Istanbul Atatürk Airport** (İstanbul Atatürk Havalimanı; *tel 0212 463 3000, ataturkairport .com),* located on the European side of the city. Discount carriers generally serve the Asian side's **Sabiha Gökçen Airport** (Sabiha Gökçen Havalimanı; *tel 0216 588 8888, sgairport.com).* Both modern airports have international and domestic terminals, banks, change facilities, and ATMs.

Taxis depart from Istanbul Atatürk Airport outside the arrivals hall. A taxi downtown takes about 40 minutes and costs around US$25. If you're traveling solo and your luggage is manageable it can be just as easy to hop aboard the 60-minute **tram** to Kabataş and all points in between. Follow the airport's red and blue "M" (Metro) signs to the **Aksaray-Airport Metro** (Aksaray-Havalimanı Hafif Metrosu). Purchase two inexpensive jetons *($):* Pop one into the turnstile to enter this line. Metros depart every few minutes, all of them heading to Aksaray. Descend at the sixth stop, Zeytinburnu, where you'll change lines. Look for signage pointing the way to the **Zeytinburnu-Kabataş Tramway** (Zeytinburnu-Kabataş Tramvayı). Insert your second jeton into the turnstile, walk down the steps to your left, and board the waiting tram.

Guests staying in Taksim are better off with the **Havaş buses** (around US$5 per person; *havas.net)* that link Atatürk Airport with Taksim Square every 30 minutes for the 45-minute ride into town.

Taxis depart from outside the Sabiha Gökçen Airport arrivals hall. A taxi heading downtown—crossing the Bosporus en route—takes an hour and costs around US$35. The **Havaş bus** journey time between Taksim and Sabiha Gökçen Airport (around US$8 per person) is also an hour. Always allow extra time for traffic delays.

GETTING AROUND

Public Transportation

Istanbul's superb public transportation system contains more than a dozen modes of transport, including funiculars, ferries, and a Metro tunnel under the Bosporus. Visitors are advised to load prepaid funds on an **İstanbulkart** (available from any newsstand; *istanbulkart .iett.gov.tr),* which they can then use to speed through the turnstiles of every transportation system in town, ferries and Nostalgic Trams included. Children aged five and under ride for free on all of Istanbul's public transportation.

By Boat

Istanbul's largest ferry company is **Hızlı Feribot İskelesi** *(ido.com.tr).* Boats depart from Eminönü, Karaköy, Üsküdar, Kabataş, and dozens of minor stations to link all points on the Bosporus. Each one combines fabulous views with an onboard tea service that will deliver you a tea *(çay)* at your chair.

By Metro, Tram, & Bus

Istanbul's Metro, tramway, and buses will get you anywhere you need to go. Just use an **İstanbulkart** (see above) transport pass, but avoid rush-hour traffic wherever possible. For Istanbul transit routes and schedules, see *iett.gov.tr.*

By Taxi

The Istanbul streets are filled with bright yellow taxis *(taksi).* They're metered and relatively inexpensive, especially if shared between three or four passengers. Make sure you state your destination clearly.

TOURS & SIGHTSEEING

Bicycle Tours

Istanbul is undergoing a cycling revolution, with bike lanes under construction alongside the entire length of the Bosporus. Cycle tour company **Istanbul On Bike** *(istanbulonbike.com)* offers cross-continental and Old City tours.

Boat Tours

The best way to appreciate the Bosporus is by boat. There are regular hop-on, hop-off public ferries that take you to all major ports around the city.

Ninety-minute and five-hour **Bosphorus Tours** (see p. 25, *$$-$$$, sehirhatlari .com and turyol.com)* depart every morning and afternoon from the Eminönü docks. These ferries cruise past the **Dolmabahçe Palace** (Dolmabahçe Sarayı; see pp. 152–153) the **Beylerbeyi Palace** (Beylerbeyi Sarayı; see p. 162), and a score of other grand waterside homes. Longer voyages include a lunch stop at Anadolu Kavağı village near the Black Sea.

Bus Tours

Taking a **Big Bus Company** *(bigbustours.com)* tour is a fine way to get your bearings. Their 24-hour tickets allow passengers to hop on and hop off the open-top tour bus anywhere from the **Beylerbeyi Palace** (Beylerbeyi Sarayı; see p. 162), to the **Grand Bazaar** (Kapalı Çarşı; see pp. 80–83).

Walking Tours

Culinary Backstreets *($$$$, culinarybackstreets.com)* lead small group tours into the most obscure foodie corners of Istanbul, including the seldom-visited suburbs of Üsküdar and Fatih, to sample delights like pit-baked lamb and clotted cream *(kaymak).*

Museum Pass İstanbul
Purchasing a three-day **Museum Pass İstanbul** *($$$$, muzekart.com)* not only gives you free entry to a selection of major museums, it will also save you an enormous amount of time. You'll bypass any lines to enter the following museums directly: the **Istanbul Archaeology Museums** (İstanbul Arkeoloji Müzeleri; see pp. 58–59); the **Great Palace Mosaic Museum** (Büyük Saray Mozaikleri Müzesi; see p. 71); **Chora Church** (Kariye Müzesi; see pp. 98–99); the **Museum of Turkish & Islamic Art** (Türk ve İslam Eserleri Müzesi; see p. 104); **Whirling Dervish Hall** (Galata Mevlevihanesi; see p. 110);

Yıldız Palace (Yıldız Sarayı; see pp. 148–49); the **Hagia Sophia** (Ayasofya Müzesi; see pp. 60–61); and **Topkapı Palace** (Topkapı Sarayı; see pp. 62–65) and its harem. The pass gives free entry and discounted access to other venues, too. Passes can be purchased at the ticket booth of any of the participating museums.

PRACTICAL ADVICE

Electricity
Turkey's electrical system operates on 220 volts/50 Hz. Electrical outlets accept plugs that have two round prongs, the same as those used in Europe. Travelers from North America and the U.K. will need an adapter.

Money Matters
Money can be changed at most—but not all—banks. In Istanbul there are change offices in the airports and along İstiklal Caddesi. Many Grand Bazaar transactions can be paid for in dollars or euros, as well as the Turkish lira (*Türk lirası, abbreviated TL*).

In Istanbul, credit (Mastercard, Visa, and American Express) and debit cards are generally accepted as payment in almost all establishments. There are also banks and ATM cashpoints on every street corner. Be sure that you know your PIN code.

Opening Times
Major tourist sights are open from 8:30 a.m. or 9 a.m. until 5:30 p.m., with later opening hours in summer. Their weekly closure is usually on Monday or Tuesday. Most banks and post offices (PTT) are open Monday–Friday, 9 a.m.–noon and 1:30–5 p.m.

Restaurants often offer continuous service, with kitchens opening for breakfast from around 8 a.m. and not closing up until after dinner, often in the early morning hours. Turks eat their evening meal late by North American standards, and popular restaurants tend to get crowded from around 9 p.m. onward. Bars and cafés stay open even later.

Shops are normally open Monday–Saturday from 10 a.m.–7 p.m., with those along Istanbul's central İstiklal Caddesi staffed until 10 p.m. or later. Larger superstores are open from 8:30 a.m.–10 p.m. Pharmacies are open Monday–Saturday from 9 a.m.–7 p.m. Each neighborhood also has a night pharmacy, usually revolving between different branches.

Post Offices
Post Offices (*PTT, ptt.gov .tr*) are dotted throughout Istanbul. Main offices in the city include **Sirkeci PTT** (*Büyük Postane, Büyük Postane Caddesi, tel 0212 526 1200*) and **Galatasaray PTT** (*İstiklal Caddesi 90, tel 0212 249 0796*). You can purchase postage stamps from here,

or from almost any store that sells postcards.

Religion
Turkey is a Sunni Muslim country, but other world religions are represented in Istanbul, including significant numbers of Greek Orthodox and Armenian Christians. There are synagogues in Galata and Balat and two prominent Catholic churches on İstiklal Caddesi.

Rest Rooms
Public restrooms (*tuvalet*) are widespread, and usually cost 1TL per person. Mosques also always have public toilets. While in many restrooms you'll encounter Western-style toilets, some are equipped with "squat" toilets. As a rule, toilet paper should always be thrown into a garbage bin that you'll find next to the toilet.

Telephones
Turks are cell phone crazy and often carry two per person. WiFi is ubiquitous and can be found in every hotel, café, and bar, so it makes sense to turn your smartphone's data roaming to "off" to avoid hefty overseas data charges.

All Turkish numbers consist of 11 digits: a four-number area code (0212 or 0216 for Istanbul), then a seven-digit number. If you are calling Turkey from abroad, dial your international access code (011 from the United States and Canada, 00 from the United Kingdom), 90 for

TRAVEL ESSENTIALS

Turkey, followed by the area code—dropping the initial 0—then the telephone number. The same system applies for cell phone numbers. To call abroad from Turkey dial 00, then the country code, area code, and telephone number. Should you need additional assistance you can reach international operators on 115.

Time Differences
All of Turkey is in the Eastern European time zone. This means that it is two hours ahead of the United Kingdom, seven hours ahead of North America's Eastern Time, and ten hours ahead of North America's Pacific Time.

Tipping
While tipping may not be traditional in Turkey, it has been enthusiastically embraced. Most hospitality workers now expect a small tip from foreigners, and leaving nothing is viewed as rude. In restaurants a tip of 10% is generous. In all other cases (cafés, bars, taxis, porters), round up the bill, or leave a couple of lira.

Travelers With Disabilities
High-end hotels and prominent tourist sights are generally outfitted with facilities for travelers with disabilities. However, not much else is. Almost all roads and sidewalks are irregular; some elevators and restrooms can be tight. That said, Turks will go out of their way to assist you in any way possible. In the United States contact **SATH** (Society for Accessible Travel & Hospitality; sath.org) before you travel; in the United Kingdom contact **RADAR** (radar.org.uk).

VISITOR INFORMATION

Useful Websites
Turkey's official tourism portal (goturkey.com) has lots of information and scores of tempting photos about every destination in Istanbul.
Turkey Travel Planner (turkeytravelplanner.com) is an excellent and informative resource written by longtime local expert Tom Brosnahan.

Tourist Offices
Local tourist offices tend to be very poorly stocked. Your hotel receptionist is likely to be far more clued up about local day trips, site opening hours, and restaurant recommendations.

EMERGENCIES

Embassies
U.S. Consulate:
İstinye Mahallesi, Kaplıcalar Mevkii 2, İstinye, Istanbul
tel 0212 335 9000
istanbul.usconsulate.gov

U.K. Consulate:
Meşrutiyet Caddesi 34, Tepebaşi, Istanbul
tel 0212 334 6400
gov.uk/government/world/turkey

Canadian Consulate:
İstiklal Caddesi 189/5, Istanbul
tel 0212 251 9838
canadainternational.gc.ca

Emergency Telephone Numbers
Ambulance 112
Fire 110
Police 155
Tourist police 0212 527 4503

Health Issues
No specific vaccinations are needed to travel to Turkey. Avoid tap water, and opt instead for bottled water. Cases of rabies are still known to exist in Istanbul. If bitten by a stray animal, head immediately to any hospital and you'll be given a free antirabies injection. For over-the-counter medication and antibiotics, pharmacies (eczane) are dotted throughout the city. Hospitals with English-speaking staff include the **American Hospital** (Amerikan Hastanesi; tel 0212 444 3777, amerikanhastanesi.org) in Nişantaşı and the **German Hospital** (Alman Hastanesi; tel 0212 293 2150) in Taksim.

Lost Property
If your passport or valuables are lost or stolen, head to the **Tourist Police** (tel 0212 527 4503) located just opposite the entrance to the **Basilica Cistern** (Yerebatan Sarnıcı; see pp. 56–57). File an official police report here, which you'll need for a replacement passport as well as for insurance purposes.

HOTELS

Hotels in Istanbul are comfy, convivial, and extremely sophisticated places to stay. In short, a classy hotel scene has simply been created in order to match Turkey's worldly, well-educated customer base. Every hotel listed here has complimentary WiFi, nonsmoking rooms, and accepts credit cards. All of these hotels can arrange a private airport pick-up service, although it's cheaper simply to hop in a cab or use public transportation.

Accommodations

Istanbul's hotels fit into four broad categories: luxury, boutique, historical, and budget. Each category tends to be concentrated in a particular area of the city. Several show-stopping luxury hotels have opened in Nişantaşı and Beşiktaş in recent years, like **Raffles** and **W Hotel.** These boast resident tour guides and award-winning restaurants. Unless exploring the lively local areas, guests usually hop in a taxi to reach the major sights.

Less expensive are the dozens of boutique hotels, such as **SuB Hotel** or **Hammamhane**, which have set up shop in the last decades. All are exclusively located in the trendy Beyoğlu and Karaköy areas: great for bookstores, clothes, and art galleries, but a 15-minute taxi or tram ride from the historical Old City. Some hip apartment hotels can also be found in these chic neighborhoods.

Istanbul's historical hotels like **Neorian** and **Empress Zoe** are similarly priced. Almost all are in the Old City—touristy, but great for sightseeing vacations. Like boutique hotels, the best ones come with an iPod dock, a marble sink, and a pillow menu. Many also have quirky rooms covered in Turkish rugs and kilims, and each one is packed with heaps of charm.

The city's budget hotels tend to be dotted throughout Beyoğlu or sprinkled along the Old City's backstreets. The ones listed here are not just clean and tidy, but innovative and special. For example, **I'Zaz** is a four-room aparthotel concept with a shared roof terrace. High-tech hostel **Bunk** also has bargain double rooms that look they like where designed by NASA. All but the most expensive hotels offer a fabulous complimentary Turkish breakfast of eggs, cheese, olives, toast, and tea.

With visitor numbers to Turkey growing each year, it's advisable to book accommodations as far in advance of your trip as possible. Visitors who reserve a hotel two months or so in advance often receive a generous "early bird" discount from the hotel website in question. It is also worth looking on some of the hotel consolidator sites that exist, such as *booking.com* or *laterooms.com*.

Alas, Istanbul is not a quiet city. Its 14 million residents will continue to eat and drink late at night then commute to work in the morning, although top hotels will always feature double-glazing and even special quiet rooms. For mobility impaired travelers, the more modern hotels of the generally flat Old City neighborhood are preferable to the bumpy sidewalks of Beyoğlu.

Price Range

An indication of the cost of a double room in high season is given by **$** signs.

$$$$$	over TL1,000
$$$$	TL500–1,000
$$$	TL350–500
$$	TL200–350
$	under TL200

Text Symbols

 No. of Guest Rooms
Public Transportation
Parking *Elevator*
Air-conditioning
Nonsmoking *Outdoor Pool*
Indoor Pool *Health Club*
Credit Cards

THE OLD CITY

Istanbul's major historical sights, including the Hagia Sophia (Ayasofya Müzesi), the Blue Mosque (Sultan Ahmet Camii), and Topkapı Palace (Topkapı Sarayı), are within walking distance of every hotel in this timeless district. Local stores and restaurants are touristy, but hotels may be packed with Old City charm.

■ FOUR SEASONS ISTANBUL AT SULTANAHMET
$$$$$
TEVKIFHANE SOKAK 1, SULTANAHMET
TEL 0212 402 3000
fourseasons.com/istanbul
Life at this former Ottoman prison is rosier now that hotel super-group Four Seasons is running the show. Rooms are simply splendid, with marble bathrooms, iPod docking stations, Bose music players, and a distinctly Asian flavor. The famed brunch every Sunday lunchtime draws Istanbul's social elite from miles around.
Gülhane *65*
All major cards

■ WHITE HOUSE HOTEL
$$$
ÇATALÇEŞME SOKAK 21, SULTANAHMET
TEL 0212 526 0019
istanbulwhitehouse.com
Amid the cluster of Sultanahmet's many hotels, the welcoming White House Hotel is a cut above the rest. Staff are friendly, and the petite Ottoman-style rooms have been decorated with care. Perfectly located for all of Istanbul's major sights; there are large discounts out of season, plus free airport pick-up for guests who are staying three days or more.
Sultanahmet *22* *All major cards*

■ HOTEL EMPRESS ZOE
$$$
ADLIYE SOKAK 10, SULTANAHMET
TEL 0212 581 2504
emzoe.com
A true boutique hotel boasting romantic rooms, many with frescoes and antique touches. Delightful garden. Prayer call audible from the neighboring Blue Mosque. Steep, narrow staircases make it unsuitable for some.
Sultanahmet *25*
All major cards

■ AYASOFYA KONAKLARI
$$$
SOĞUKÇEŞME SOKAK, SULTANAHMET
TEL 0212 513 3660
ayasofyapensions.com
A historical hotel set in a row of traditional wooden townhouses by the Hagia Sophia, with a sumptuous private garden to the rear.

This tranquil retreat has nine British country-house-styled rooms, several of which hosted Queen Sophia of Spain on her visit to Istanbul.
Gülhane *9*
All major cards

■ HOTEL IBRAHIM PASHA
$$$
TERZIHANE SOKAK 7, SULTANAHMET
TEL 0212 518 0394
ibrahimpasha.com
A sleek hotel that blends its 19th-century origins with open fireplaces, contemporary furniture, plus a DVD and book library. Head up from the designer foyer and guest-only bar to stylish, peaceful, quiet rooms. A rooftop terrace overlooks the Blue Mosque.
Sultanahmet *24*
All major cards

■ HOTEL AMIRA
$$
MUSTAFAPAŞA SOKAK 79, SULTANAHMET
TEL 0212 516 1640
hotelamira.com
An upscale spot in the heart of Istanbul's Old City. Rooms feature stylish yet cozy modern decor; bathrooms are equipped with rain showers or Jacuzzi tubs. Aside from the quiet location a key attraction is the stunning seaview rooftop.
Sultanahmet *32*
All major cards

■ BERCE HOTEL
$-$$
MUSTAFAPAŞA SOKAK 6, SULTANAHMET
TEL 0212 518 8883
bercehotel.com

HOTELS

Top value, just a few hundred yards from all the Old City's attractions, including the Blue Mosque and Hagia Sophia. Rooms are modern, but the Berce's big pull is its panoramic terrace where guests can both breakfast and/or enjoy an aperitif in view of the Bosporus.
🏨 *Sultanahmet* 🚹 7 🅂
🅂 *All major cards*

■ APRICOT HOTEL
$
AMIRAL TAFDIL SOKAK 22, SULTANAHMET
TEL 0212 638 1658
hotelapricot.com
You get what you pay for at this fine, friendly budget hotel within striking distance of all Sultanahmet's sights. Its modern rooms may be small, but some boast views over the Bosporus.
🏨 *Sultanahmet* 🚹 6 🖃🅂
🅂 *All major cards*

GRAND BAZAAR TO EMINÖNÜ

There are few hotels in this action-packed commercial neighborhood. But most of these are just a stroll away from Eminönü's Bosporus ferry port.

■ NEORION HOTEL
$$$
ORHANIYE SOKAK 14, EMINÖNÜ
TEL 0212 527 9090
neorionhotel.com
Superbly located hotel that takes customer service to new heights. Refresh yourself in

the opulent Ottoman-themed rooms and Finnish sauna, then wander straight out to Istanbul's major sights. A glass of Turkish Chardonnay on the roof terrace makes for an enviable Facebook update.
🏨 *Sirkeci* 🚹 54 🖃🅂🏊🅂
🍷🅂 *All major cards*

■ SIRKECI MANSION
$$$
TAYA HATUN SOKAK 5, EMINÖNÜ
TEL 0212 528 4344
sirkecimansion.com
An award-winning hotel with on-site hamam and spa, plus a rooftop sun terrace. Classy rooms come with pillow menus plus tea- and coffee-making facilities. Restaurants include rooftop Neyzade for classic Anatolian cuisine.
🏨 *Sirkeci* 🚹 32 🖃🅂🏊🅂
🅂 *All major cards*

■ DIVANI ALI HOTEL
$$
DIVANI ALI SOKAK 7, BEYAZIT-GRAND BAZAAR
TEL 0212 638 1200
divanialihotel.com
Great value Ottoman-themed splendor on a 150-year-old street. Dip into the irresistible rooftop Jacuzzi after a shopping tour of the Grand Bazaar—just a two-minute stroll away.
🏨 *Beyazit* 🚹 32 🖃🅂🏊🅂
🅂 *All major cards*

■ HOTEL NILES
$$
DIBEKLI CAMI SOKAK 19, BEYAZIT-GRAND BAZAAR
TEL 0212 517 3239
hotelniles.com

A finely renovated family-run hotel in a 19th-century townhouse. Take tea on the indoor terrace of the elegant lobby, or amid the jungle of plants on the roof, where a fabulous breakfast is also served. Early bird bookings make the Niles one of Istanbul's best bargains.
🏨 *Beyazit* 🚹 39 🖃🅂🏊🅂
🅂 *All major cards*

SOUTHERN GOLDEN HORN

History fans will be among the tourists who choose to stay in this timeless residential zone.

■ KARIYE HOTEL
$$
KARIYE CAMII SOKAK 6, EDIRNEKAPI
TEL 0212 534 8414
kariyeotel.com
A great-value hotel nestled up against the Chora Museum and the crumbling sites of Fatih. Rooms in this renovated 19th-century villa possess old Ottoman charm—wooden bedsteads and antique reading lamps included.
🏨 *Edirnekapı* Metro 🚹 26
🅿🅂🏊🅂🅂 *All major cards*

■ EDUCA SUITES
$
HIZIR ÇAVUŞ ÇIÇEKLI BOSTAN SOKAK 20, BALAT
TEL 0212 533 2503
educasuites.com
Historians and city strollers flock to this snug hotel in the backstreets of the age-old Balat quarter. A short

TRAVEL ESSENTIALS

walk from a dozen ancient churches, plus an array of locals-only restaurants and teashops.

🚌 Buses 35D, 48E, 55T, 99A
� 32 📶 💳 ♿ All major cards

GALATA & KARAKÖY

Karaköy is currently the hippest suburb in all Istanbul. A dozen boutique hotels look onto its pavement cafés. Galata has a similarly chic hotel selection.

■ VAULT
$$$
BANKALAR CADDESI 5, KARAKÖY
TEL 0212 244 3400
thehousehotel.com
Istanbul's former Deutsche Bank headquarters were built in 1867, and transformed into this excellent boutique hotel in 2014. Original tiles and stone steps are paired with hardwood floors and marble bathrooms. The bar's cocktail cabinet, housed in an ancient bank vault, is the finest touch.

🚌 Karaköy K 63 ⛴ 📶 💳 ♿ All major cards

■ ISTANBUL SWEET HOME
$$$
VARIOUS LOCATIONS, GALATA
NO PHONE
istanbulsweethome.com
These ten exquisite, managed apartments are dotted around Beyoğlu's most charmingly antique areas. All are well equipped with WiFi, full kitchens, period features, and much else besides. Some even feature Turkish hamams, panoramic terraces, and entire libraries. Almost all work out cheaper than a hotel equivalent if booked by the week.

🚌 Tünel 🚈 12
♿ All major cards

■ SUB HOTEL
$$
NECATIBEY CADDESI 91, KARAKÖY
TEL 0212 243 0005
subkarakoy.com
SuB is emblematic of the ultrahip Karaköy neighborhood. It opened in 2014, a stone's throw from Istanbul Modern and a dozen cool restaurants. Each room features a custom-made steel bed and a designer bathroom. Knowledgeable local staff offer insider tips on what to see, where to eat, and what to buy in the city. Unwind in the hotel's rooftop bar at the end of the day.

🚌 Tophane 🚈 17 ⛴ 📶 🏊 ♿ All major cards

■ PORTUS HOUSE
$-$$
MUMHANE CADDESI 31, KARAKÖY
TEL 0212 292 3850
portushouse.com
A carefully curated selection of smart modern rooms inside an art nouveau townhouse. The tram, Karaköy ferry, and Istanbul Modern are all a three-minute stroll away.

🚌 Tophane 🚈 10 ⛴ 📶 🏊 ♿ All major cards

THE HEART OF BEYOĞLU

Lords, ladies, and elegant travelers have bedded down in Beyoğlu since time immemorial. It still boasts the city's best collection of hotels, bars, and high-end shops.

■ PERA PALACE
$$$$$
MEŞRUTIYET CADDESI 52, BEYOĞLU
TEL 0212 377 4000
perapalace.com
Even a cocktail at the Pera Palace will bring you face-to-face with history. Such luminaries as female spy Mata Hari, British author Agatha Christie, and the Turkish Republic's founding father Atatürk all stayed here. This once creaking grande dame hotel was refreshed by high-end Arabian operator Jumeirah. Elegant dining options include the refined Franco-Turkish Agatha Restaurant, a patisserie, and the classic Orient Bar.

🚌 Tünel 🚈 115 🅿 ⛴ 📶 🏊 🍽 ♿ All major cards

■ WITT SUITES
$$$$
DEFTERDAR YOKUŞU 26, CIHANGIR, BEYOĞLU
TEL 0212 293 1500
wittistanbul.com
Seventeen mind-blowingly luxurious rooms that have been voted some of Istanbul's finest by travelers and magazines alike. Rooms are giant—at least 600 square feet (60 sq m) open-plan

creations with walk-in
wetrooms, six-headed rain
showers, and center-room
kitchenettes with just the right
equipment to mix a vodka
martini. Jaw-droppingly cool.

🚇 Tophane 🕐 17 ⬆ Ⓢ 🏊
🎮 🔑 All major cards

■ TOMTOM SUITES
$$$$
TOMTOM KAPTAN SOKAK 18,
BEYOĞLU
TEL 0212 292 494
tomtomsuites.com

What started life as an
outbuilding of the nearby
French Embassy is now a
Nordic-style boutique palace.
This suite-only hotel is replete
with handmade furniture,
art-filled walls, rain showers,
a vast literature and music
library, and some astounding
Bosporus views.

🚇 Tophane 🕐 15 ⬆ Ⓢ 🏊
🎮 🔑 All major cards

■ THE HOUSE HOTEL
$$$
BOSTANBAŞI CADDESI 19,
BEYOĞLU
TEL 0212 244 3400
thehousehotel.com

This 1890s mansion in
Beyoğlu was converted
into an extraordinarily
hip collection of suites by
Istanbul's leading design
agency, Autoban. Parisian-
style interiors, art deco
sinks, parquet floors, and
chandeliers blend with
high linen counts and
exemplary service.

🚇 Tophane 🕐 25 ⬆ Ⓢ
🏊 🔑 All major cards

■ MAMA SHELTER
$$
ISTIKLAL CADDESI 50, BEYOĞLU
TEL 0212 343 0095
mamashelter.com/istanbul

Istanbul's designer bargain
opened in 2013 to deliver
industrial chic guestrooms
for under $150 per night
atop İstiklal Caddesi's main
shopping mall. The best bit is
a so-cool-it-hurts lobby and
breakfast room where you
can post a cell phone selfie
of yourself on a dozen digital
TV screens. It's as friendly as
it is fun.

🚇 Taksim 🕐 81 ⬆ Ⓢ 🏊
🔑 All major cards

■ I'ZAZ
$$
BALIK SOKAK 12, BEYOĞLU
TEL 0212 252 1382
izaz.com

An ultrahip loft living concept,
with a chic one-bedroom
apartment on each floor.
Mod cons include designer
bathrooms, hardwood
furniture, and ultrafast WiFi
players. Guests share a
rooftop terrace that overlooks
the British Consulate gardens,
and a communal kitchen. The
apartments are two blocks
from İstiklal Caddesi.

🚇 Tünel 4 ⬆ Ⓢ 🎮 📺
🔑 All major cards

■ PERADAYS
$$
HAMALBAŞI CADDESI 32,
BEYOĞLU
TEL 0212 245 1270
peradays.com

Easily Beyoğlu's most
charming B&B. Ultrastylish
contemporary rooms occupy

a renovated 19th-century
townhouse. The nine suites
benefit from award-winning
service, plus a top-floor
terrace where guests can
take their expansive Turkish
breakfast or sink a sundowner.

🚇 Taksim 🕐 9 ⬆ Ⓢ
🔑 All major cards

■ BUNK TAKSIM
$
PAPA RONCALLI SOKAK 34,
TAKSIM
TEL 0212 343 0095
bunkhostels.com

Even fashion bible *Elle*
magazine is a fan of this
Anglo-German-Turkish
creation: a hip hostel with
ultrastylish communal
bathrooms, plus private
double rooms for couples
and families. This bargain
operation also includes a
pizzeria and a cinema room.
There is another branch near
the British Consulate on
İstiklal Caddesi.

🚇 Taksim 🕐 45 Ⓢ 🏊
🔑 All major cards

BOSPORUS &
NIŞANTAŞI

The city's swishest suburbs
are home to the city's chicest
hotels. The downside? The
city's main historical sights
and public transportation are
generally a taxi ride away.

■ RAFFLES
$$$$$
ZORLU CENTER, ZINCIRLIKUYU
TEL 0212 924 0200
raffles.com/istanbul

Since 2014 this astounding address has laid rightful claim to the title of Istanbul's finest hotel. Overlooking almost 14 million of the city's residents from its hilltop locale, it contains a 33,000-square-foot (3,000 sq m) spa, a restaurant run by a two-star Michelin chef, and enough butlers to give *Downton Abbey* a run for its money. Their first guest was Lady Gaga.

🚇 *Gayrettepe* 🛏 185 🅿 ⬆ 🌀 ❄ 🏊 📺 🗝 *All major cards*

■ PARK HYATT ISTANBUL —MAÇKA PALAS
$$$$
BRONZ SOKAK 4, NIŞANTAŞI
TEL 0212 315 1234
istanbul.park.hyatt.com
Nişantaşı's Maçka Palas is a magnificent art deco edifice, constructed by Milanese architects in 1922. One of Istanbul's most refined offerings (although the even more upscale Grand Hyatt lies near Taksim Square), it couples luxury, period-style rooms with iPod docks and lashings of walnut wood and marble.

🚇 *Osmanbey* 🛏 90 🅿 ⬆ 🌀 ❄ 🏊 📺 🗝 *All major cards*

■ W ISTANBUL
$$$
SÜLEYMAN SEBA CADDESI 22, BEŞIKTAŞ
TEL 0212 381 2121
wistanbul.com.tr
Totally unique, and one of Istanbul's hippest hotels. The lavishly cool rooms feature 350-thread linen count bedspreads, marble sinks, and Ottoman loungers. Some rooms even have private gardens, outdoor cabanas, or their own rooftop terrace. The decadently trendy W Lounge bar and restaurant is on site.

🚢 *Beşiktaş Ferry Terminal* 🛏 136 ⬆ 🌀 ❄ 🏊 🗝 *All major cards*

■ PANCALDI SUITES
$$
TAY SOKAK 3, NIŞANTAŞI
TEL 0212 241 2694
pancaldisuites.com
A small townhouse hotel with wooden floors, alcove sofas, bare-brick walls, and fine Turkish linen, in the heart of Istanbul's shopaholic suburb. More importantly, elegant owner Fulya knows every Nişantaşı address for the best boutiques and eats in the quarter.

🚇 *Osmanbey* 🛏 4 🌀 ❄ 🗝 *All major cards*

ASIAN ISTANBUL

The few hotels that exist in Asian Istanbul are generally tranquil, upscale, and unashamedly elegant.

■ SUMAHAN ON THE WATER
$$$$$
KULELI CADDESI 43, ÇENGELKÖY
TEL 0216 422 8000
sumahan.com
Once a rakı distillery before its reincarnation as a fabulous boutique hotel, Sumahan is an elegant arrangement of suites, dining terraces, a wellness center, and even a traditional hamam, right on the Bosporus. Their private launch lies ready to whisk you across to Europe.

🚢 *Çengelköy Ferry Terminal* 🛏 20 🅿 🌀 ❄ 🗝 *All major cards*

■ AKIN SUITES
$$
KIRMIZI KUŞAK SOKAK 18, KADIKÖY
akinsuites.com
TEL 0216 405 1370
This collection of designer suite apartments lies in the heart of Kadıköy, just two minutes from the ferry terminal and fish market. Guests may cook their own dinner at home, then feast on a knockout breakfast in the communal dining room and lounge.

🚢 *Kadıköy Ferry Terminal* 🛏 18 🌀 ❄ 🗝 *All major cards*

■ JULIET ROOMS & KITCHEN
$
ŞIFA SOKAK 31 MODA
julietistanbul.com
TEL 0216 348 7000
Bucolically sited on a tree-lined boulevard near the bakeries, bars, and restaurants of the upscale Moda neighborhood. Guests should expect a tidy guestroom with a marble shower, plus homemade lemonade and muffins at breakfast.

🚢 *Kadıköy Ferry Terminal* 🛏 14 🌀 ❄ 🗝 *All major cards*

MENU **READER**

Breakfast

gözleme Thin, savory breakfast pancake, usually stuffed with cheese, spinach, or potatoes.

menemen Eggs scrambled with tomatoes, onions, and sweet green peppers.

Starters and Meze

börek Layered pastry stuffed with vegetables, cheese, or meat.

cacık Cool "soup" of yogurt, cucumber, garlic, and mint.

çorba Soup: The most popular variations are *mercimek çorbası* (lentils and vegetables) and *ezogelin çorbası* (bulgur, red lentils, and mint).

meze A selection of small sharing platters; *soğuk mezeler* (cold meze) are served first, followed by *sıcak mezeler* (hot meze).

mücver Zucchini and white cheese fritters.

peynir Standard word for cheese; more specific types are *beyaz peynir* (white cheese, similar to soft feta), *kaşar* (yellow, more mature cheese).

salata Salad.

turşu Pickles.

yaprak dolması Stuffed vine leaves.

zeytinyağlı Seasonal vegetables cooked in olive oil.

Breads

lahmacun Flatbread topped with ground lamb, parsley, and chili pepper.

lavaş Large, paper-thin bread.

pide Oblong flatbread, usually topped with cheese.

Main Courses

balık Fish; popular local types include *ahtapot* (octopus), *barbunya* (red mullet), *çupra* (sea bream), *hamsi* (anchovies), *kalamar* (squid), *kalkan* (turbot), *karides* (shrimp), *levrek* (sea bass), *midye* (mussels), and *uskumru* (mackerel).

güveç Casserole, cooked in a terra-cotta dish of the same name.

hünkar beğendi Lamb served atop a smoky eggplant purée.

imam bayıldı Eggplant stuffed with tomatoes, onions, and herbs.

kebabs Grilled lamb; however there are literally hundreds of versions of Turkey's most famous dish, including *döner* (slow-roasted on a spit), *İskender* (topped with foaming butter, tomato sauce, and cream), *patlıcan* (interspersed with eggplant), and *şiş kebab* (on a skewer).

köfte Meatballs, normally a mix of lamb and beef; other popular variations include *çiğ köfte* (raw beef or lamb with bulgur) and *mercimek köfte* (a vegetarian version with red lentils).

mantı Stuffed pasta, similar to ravioli and usually topped with a garlicky yogurt sauce.

Desserts *(tatlı)*

aşure Sweet pudding made from wheat, beans, dried fruits, and nuts.

baklava Sweet, syrupy, layered pastry, usually containing chopped *antep fıstığı* (pistachios) or *ceviz* (walnuts).

helva Sweet butter, flour, and sugar treat.

kabak tatlısı Dessert of pumpkin stewed in sugar syrup.

lokum Turkish delight.

sütlaç Rice pudding.

Drinks

ayran Thin, salty yogurt drink.

bira Beer

çay Tea

kahve Coffee; note that *türk kahvesi* (Turkish coffee) must be ordered *az şekerli* (with a little sugar), *şekerli* (with sugar) or *şekersiz* (without sugar).

su Water

şarap Wine; *kırmızı* (red), *beyaz* (white).

Pronunciation Guide

Here are some tips to help with Turkish pronunciation:

ı is similar to e in chicken

ö is similar to the o in word

ü is similar to the ew in chew

ç is similar to the ch in chance

ğ is similar to the k in khaki

ş is similar to the sh in shin

In addition, the letters **c, j, g** are pronounced differently from the ways they are pronounced in English:

c is similar to the j in jacket and jam

j is a soft j, similar to the French *je*.

g is pronounced as a hard g, as in give and get.

INDEX

TRAVEL ESSENTIALS

INDEX

INDEX

CREDITS

Walking Istanbul
Tristan Rutherford & Kathryn Tomasetti

Published by the National Geographic Society
Gary E. Knell, *President and Chief Executive Officer*
John M. Fahey, *Chairman of the Board*
Declan Moore, *Chief Media Officer*
Chris Johns, *Chief Content Officer*

Prepared by the Book Division
Hector Sierra, *Senior Vice President and General Manager*
Lisa Thomas, *Senior Vice President and Editorial Director*
Jonathan Halling, *Creative Director*
Marianne R. Koszorus, *Design Director*
Barbara A. Noe, *Senior Editor*
R. Gary Colbert, *Production Director*
Jennifer A. Thornton, *Director of Managing Editorial*
Susan S. Blair, *Director of Photography*
Meredith C. Wilcox, *Director, Administration and Rights Clearance*

Staff for This Book
Allie Fahey, *Editorial Assistant*
Elisa Gibson, *Art Director*
Debbie Gibbons, *Director of Intracompany and Custom Cartography*
Mapping Specialists, Ltd., *Map Research and Production*
Marshall Kiker, *Associate Managing Editor*
Mike O'Connor, *Production Editor*
Mike Horenstein, *Production Manager*
Rock Wheeler, *Rights Clearance Specialist*
Katie Olsen, *Design Production Specialist*
Nicole Miller, *Design Production Assistant*
Bobby Barr, *Manager, Production Services*
Rebekah Cain, *Imaging*

Created by Toucan Books Ltd
Ellen Dupont, *Editorial Director*
Anna Southgate, *Editor*
Dave Jones, *Designer*
Sharon Southren, *Picture Research*
Özgün Özçers, *Editorial Support*
Merritt Cartographic, *Maps*
Marion Dent, *Proofreader*
Marie Lorimer, *Indexer*

The information in this book has been carefully checked and to the best of
our knowledge is accurate. However, details are subject to change, and the
National Geographic Society cannot be responsible for such changes, or for
errors or omissions. Assessments of sites, hotels, and restaurants are based
on the author's subjective opinions, which do not necessarily reflect the
publisher's opinion.

The National Geographic Society is one of the world's largest nonprofit
scientific and educational organizations. Founded in 1888 to "increase and
diffuse geographic knowledge," the member-supported Society works to
inspire people to care about the planet. Through its online community,
members can get closer to explorers and photographers, connect with
other members around the world, and help make a difference. National
Geographic reflects the world through its magazines, television
programs, films, music and radio, books, DVDs, maps, exhibitions, live
events, school publishing programs, interactive media, and merchandise.
National Geographic magazine, the Society's official journal, published
in English and 38 local-language editions, is read by more than 60
million people each month. The National Geographic Channel reaches
440 million households in 171 countries in 38 languages. National
Geographic Digital Media receives more than 25 million visitors a month.
National Geographic has funded more than 10,000 scientific research,
conservation, and exploration projects and supports an education
program promoting geography literacy. For more information, visit www
.nationalgeographic.com.

For more information, please call 1-800-NGS LINE
(647-5463) or write to the following address:

National Geographic Society
1145 17th Street NW
Washington, D.C. 20036-4688 U.S.A.

Your purchase supports our nonprofit work and makes you part of our
global community. Thank you for sharing our belief in the power of
science, exploration, and storytelling to change the world. To activate
your member benefits, complete your free membership profile at
natgeo.com/joinnow.

For information about special discounts for bulk purchases,
please contact National Geographic Books Special Sales:
ngspecsales@ngs.org

For rights or permissions inquiries, please contact National Geographic
Books Subsidiary Rights: ngbookrights@ngs.org

ISBN: 978-1-4262-1636-7

Printed in Hong Kong
15/THK/1